Glass Fusing

BOOK ONE

WRITTEN BY
Boyce Lundstrom and Daniel Schwoerer

Boyce Lundstrom   *Daniel W. Schwoerer*

PUBLISHED BY
VITREOUS PUBLICATIONS, INC.

Published by Vitreous Publications, Inc.

© 1983 Vitreous Publications, Inc.

Library of Congress Catalog Card
Number 83-050657

ISBN Number 0-9612282-0-2

Edited by Lola M. Salmonson

Designed by
Nancy Olson

Fusing Ranch photographs by
David Wittkop

1. *(Cover photo)* Ruth Brockmann.
Group of fused and sagged masks show-
ing variety of techniques and the expanse
of her fusible color palette.

2. *(Title page photo)* Boyce Lundstrom.
Red glass fused bowl using first Bullrods
produced by Bullseye Glass Company in
1979. Piece was slumped through a metal
flange ring.

TABLE OF CONTENTS

INTRODUCTION

We are entering an exciting new era in the 4000-year history of glass. Twentieth-century technology makes it attractive for artists and craftpersons to find a medium of expression in ancient glass processes. Kiln technology, lightweight refractories, the silicon chip, and other modern engineering innovations make a return to old processes, such as glass fusing, practical and not limited to the production of functional objects or other time-honored forms. Exploration into the full potential of glass as a material has never been as exciting or as accessible as it is today.

This book endeavors to point out that glass fusing is within the realm of the individual artist and craftsperson. All that is necessary is a sense of design, an inquisitive mind, and the willingness and drive required to build or buy the needed equipment. Our intention is to share the collective information acquired by us over the past nine years at Bullseye Glass Company, and in particular, the last two years in the development of fused glass.

During these two years, Bullseye developed a reliable system for testing fusing compatibility. This has led to the production of a palette of fusible colors of glass ranging across the visible spectrum. It is partly from this achievement that the stimulus of this book has been derived. The potential of fused glass and the belief that the decade of the eighties will signal a return to the creative exploitation of fusing colored glasses have provided the remaining stimulus in the preparation of this book.

The information herein is concerned only with the basics of fusing glass and is not to be considered a complete reference for either advanced forming techniques or advanced technical data. The basics discussed are intended to turn the individual on to the idea that he can create anything he so desires with glass. Neither history nor the present should be controlling factors. It is hoped the artist will then develop personal techniques for specific results as he explores the almost endless possibilities for glass forming through the fusing and slumping processes. With the exception of a few technical journals, no concise book is available on fusing and laminating which fully explains the basic knowledge required to achieve continuing success. All books written about this subject contain conclusions of dubious value from personal observations, and none approaches the process of fusing colored glass which is scientifically well founded. Standards currently do not exist for either the fusing process or the glasses that are considered fusible. Bullseye Glass Company is attempting to write a new language as it applies to the technology of fusing and laminating together different colored glasses by the application of heat.

Students and professionals of the present flat stained glass movement will now have the opportunity to be liberated by hot glass forming... designing without the black cartoon lines... producing colors and depths in glass not possible until now by using this new fusing language. We hope your creative and personal exploration in the area of fused glass will be fun, challenging, and rewarding.

4

5

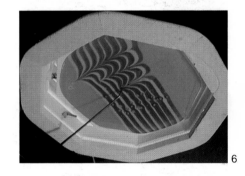
6

3. Gil Reynolds. *Fused piece with enamels.*

4-5. *Chapter 6, volume control.*

6. *Chapter 15, combing molten glass.*

7. The Corning Museum of Glass. *Inlay cane (eye); mosaic glass technique. Egypt, 19th to 21st dynasty (1304-1080 B.C.) or possibly later. L: 3.0 cm.*

8. The Corning Museum of Glass. *Fused mosaic plaque. Probably Alexandria, Egypt, 1st century B.C.-1st century A.D. L: 2.8 cm.*

HISTORY

CHAPTER 1

Many references to the origins of glass forming place the time around 2000 B.C. This specific date may be argued by historians, but it makes little difference in the context of this book. The Egyptians and Romans were undoubtedly the most advanced glass formers, and many examples of their work exist in museums around the world. In this country the Corning Museum in Corning, New York has an excellent collection of ancient fused glass pieces, some examples of which are seen on the following pages. It is from studying these early glass objects that the use of the fusing process is documented.

Many intricate bowls, beautiful jewelry, and decorative wall tiles were created by using the fusing method from approximately 1500 B.C. to approximately 500 A.D. But what happened after that to fused glass objects?

Perhaps this question can be answered by noting that glass blowing became the more immediate and desired forming method. The period from 500 A.D. to the early 1900's appears rather devoid of fused glass objects, with the exception of the "Pate de Verre" process. Pate de Verre (fusing crushed glass in a mold) was popular during the Art Nouveau period. The work of Henri Gros was representative of this type of fusing between 1880 and 1920.

The glass blowers of the early era did use some fusing techniques to apply designs to their vessels; however, their main activity was toward greater blowing knowledge for the ever-increasing utilitarian market for glass. Given this priority, it is understandable that fusing has taken so long to flourish once again as an art form.

Glass technology went through its greatest growth during and after the Renaissance in Europe. But for some reason, the fusing process did not experience the rebirth that one would have expected in this highly enlightened period. Somehow

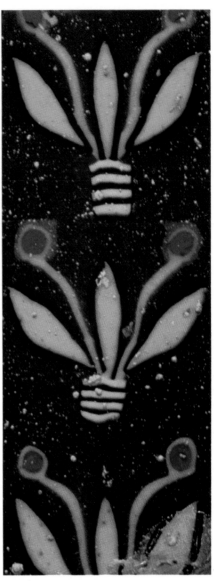

10

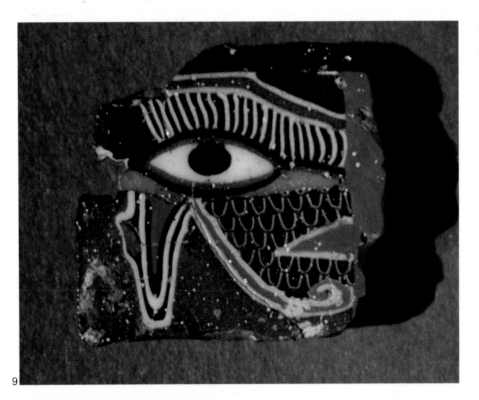

9

9. The Corning Museum of Glass. *Inlay plaque; mosaic glass technique. Roman Empire, probably Egypt. ca. 1st century B.C. –1st century A.D. H: 1.9 cm.*

10. The Corning Museum of Glass. *Inlay: mosaic glass technique. Roman Empire, probably Egypt, ca. 1st century B.C.-1st century A.D. H: 7.7 cm.*

11

12

fusing was either overlooked or ignored. Even during modern times, fusing has not experienced the growth other glass forming processes have enjoyed. Although the first 2000 years of the 4000-year existence of glass forming was rich with the use of fusing, the last 2000 years appear quite devoid of fusing.

L.C. Tiffany may have used fused glass in his master works, but not in the sense that we refer to fusing in this book. His glass was made by fusing stringers and confetti chips into the surface using hand-blowing techniques.He also designed with pieces that had been blown and then slumped flat after flower or textural designs had been applied to the surface. Frederick Carder (founder of Steuben) experimented with fused glass; however, no significant body of fused glass work was ever produced by Steuben.

Around the year 1935 glass enameling, glass slumping, and occasionally glass fusing re-appeared. Glass was abundant in many forms from inexpensive window glass to colored bottles,including Kokomo, Wissmach, and Blenko glass. The direction of this resurgence in hot glass forming was varied and developed in small clusters in local areas across the United States. The understanding of glass technology and the knowledge of working glass were not characteristic of this movement.

Historically it is time (in fact, overdue) for fusing to re-appear. New flat glass companies will publish their findings, and colored glass will be an integral part of this new information leading to the glass awareness that is now, at last, coming of age.

11. The Corning Museum of Glass. Fragment (wall revetment); cast and mosaic glass technique. Roman Empire; late 1st century B.C.-1st century A.D. L: 7.5 cm.

12. The Corning Museum of Glass. Bowl; mosaic glass technique or millefiore. Roman Empire, mid to late 1st century A.D.

13. The Corning Museum of Glass. Hawks head; cast and mosaic glass technique. Egypt, Ptolemaic, 3rd-1st century B.C. H: 4.3 cm.

14. Frances and Michael Higgins. Sculptured piece that took advantage of an accident. First made as an assembly for a 16" platter, the bottom sheet was shattered. The Higginses liked the result so much they deliberately reproduced the final piece from scratch.

13

CONTEMPORARY WORK

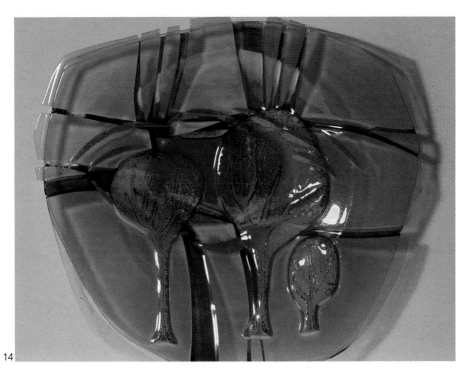

CHAPTER 2

14

15

16

Contemporary Work and Thought

We have selected approximately twenty contemporary artists to represent various aspects of the fusing medium in this book. The availability of knowledge and the openness of most glass fusers have enabled this field to advance very rapidly. Glass conventions such as PORTCON and organizations such as Glass Art Society have greatly accelerated the dissemination of this knowledge. Many new artists today are producing dynamic fused works which are greater in size and complexity than ever before seen.

In the 1940's, Michael and Frances Higgins were among the very few who chose hot glass forming, fusing, and enameling as a livelihood—first in the craft world, then in the art world. Today, they continue to make a profession out of their toils and labors.

Kay Kinney authored a book, "Glass Craft," in 1962 relating her personal experiments with the hot-working of flat glass. Kay's joy of creating with found objects and her seemingly endless enthusiasm was a bright spot for many in the glass craft movement of the early 60's.

Another artist noted in the development of glass fusing is Harriet Anderson. In 1961 she took a course in glass from Maurice Heaton at the Rochester Institute of Technology which inspired her to leave the textile craft field to explore the sparsely documented field of kiln-fired glass. The results of her many experiments and carefully recorded research over the years provided her with the resources used in publishing her notable book, "Kiln-Fired Glass," in 1970.

Achieving a usable object by fusing, enameling, or laminating glass has been a constant problem to many would-be hot glass workers. Failure comes soon to most. All of the people we mentioned above experienced problems with fusing a range of colored glasses. Consequently, they either concentrated on a very limited

15. Frances and Michael Higgins. *Sculptured vase made by heating a carefully calculated assembly of glass on a ring mold of primed clay. The glass was allowed to sag through until it fell upon and spread slightly over the kiln shelf. It was then frozen by opening the kiln when the precisely desired form was achieved (known as "drop-out" technique). The veils, which hang about the stem of the shape, go on the mold first (with spaces between them).*

16. Frances and Michael Higgins. *Fused and enameled plate, 15 inch diameter.*

17

color palette or chose to use enamels and frits on window glass.

Antique collecting in the 1960's brought about a renewed interest in stained glass. Cities such as Denver, Colorado became trading centers for stained glass windows removed from old East Coast houses and buildings. The demand for turn-of-the-century stained glass encouraged studios to create works ranging from Tiffany reproductions to contemporary designs.

The rapid growth of new stained glass studios across the country, brought about by the demand for stained glass, was made possible by a new breed of glass manufacturers and by the influence of the earlier contemporary glass blowing movement proliferated by such people as H.K. Littleton at the University of Wisconsin. Bullseye Glass Company, started by three glass blowers in 1974, was the first of its kind to fill the growing needs of the colored flat glass movement. It was followed by as many as sixteen new manufacturers in the late 70's.

The modern stained glass movement, started by mimicking the traditional turn-of-the-century work, has evolved into a very diverse art form exhibiting many original designs. The techniques of leading, foiling, beveling, sagging, enameling, casting, and pressing are being successfully exploited in a contemporary fashion. Out of this diverse and expansive effort, we see that fusing is beginning a new cycle . . . the first new major cycle in 2000 years of glass forming.

17. *Klaus Moje laying up one of his pieces.*

18. Klaus Moje. *The feather pattern was made by sawing pre-fused sections, re-arranging, and re-fusing.*

18

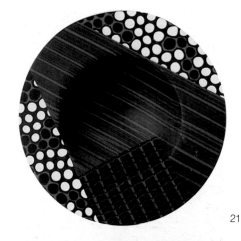

21

22

19

20

19. Klaus Moje. *Bowl made with color pattern bars. White and black color bars are used in the same method as shown in Figure 22. The six-sided polygons are not noticeable because all color bars had a black outer perimeter.*

20. Klaus Moje. *Bowl made by setting 1/8"x 3/8" strips on edge, side by side, fused together.*

21. Klaus Moje. *Fused and slumped bowl made with previously assembled pieces, laid up into a new pattern.*

22. Klaus Moje. *Bowl using color bars that have been sliced into discs, laid up touching each other, fused, and sagged. Notice how the originally round disc forms a six-sided polygon when the glass flows to fill the interstices.*

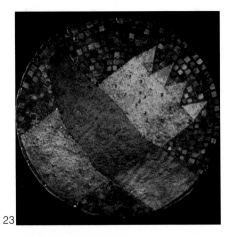

23

24

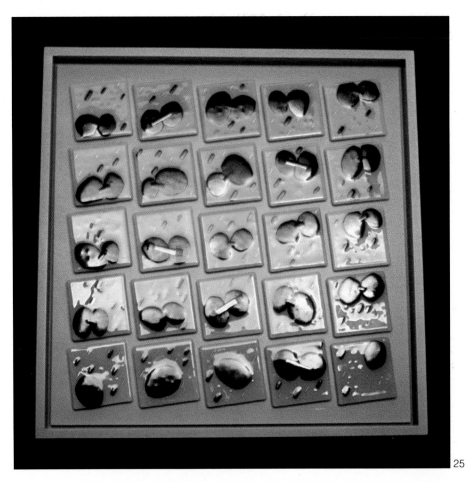

25

26

23. Liz Mapelli. *18" circle mosaic technique laid up with design down, using fiber paper instead of shelf primer to achieve greater depth in iridescent reflections.*

24. Liz Mapelli. *Fused glass tile using iridescent glass.*

25. Liz Mapelli. *24" square, 1982. Fused independent panel made for Kaiser Medical Building.*

26. Liz Mapelli. *Detail of Figure 25, using iridescent glass over Bullseye #111, fully fused but not flat. Greater surface tension of iridescent glass helps achieve dimensional effect.*

27. Liz Mapelli. *Architectural installation of the Portland Justice Center, combining fused glass tiles and Italian glass smalti.*

28. Liz Mapelli. *Detail of tiles in Portland Justice Center.*

27

29

29. Liz Mapelli. *Looking down the arcade of Portland Justice Center, showing vaulted ceiling structure before the building was completed.*

Historically, glass has been used as an architectural material. These uses included windows, wall coverings (mosaics), and floors. Now, in the 20th century, fused glass re-emerges, worthy of consideration as an architectural material. Its brilliance, durability, variety of color and texture, as well as its translucency make it a flexible and desirable medium for use in structures.

"I found that the modular pieces worked very well in an architectural setting, but were difficult to install at the gallery level, and so began creating pieces that were not only easier to hang, but also included a wide variety of techniques. Using fused glass now as an attachment, vitrolite, sandblasted imagery, oil pigment, and non-glass materials became my palette as well.

"I generally do large, fairly quick drawings and use a cut-and-paste method to arrange and re-arrange shapes and planes, and to introduce color and texture. Rhythm and pattern are important considerations in my work, and this method helps me to achieve their incorporation into each piece. Sometimes I attach the glass to the drawing I am working on, or draw directly on the glass itself as I go along. I like to work very quickly and I like a single process rather than a string of complicated steps. I prefer to make large scale, site-specific works, and currently I am using fused glass techniques in combination with other glass and non-glass materials."

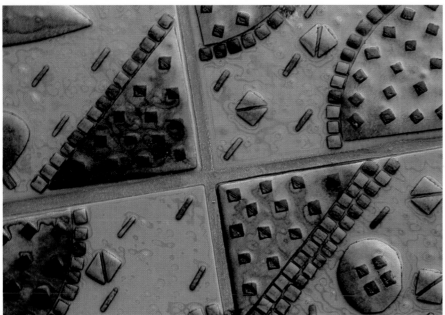

28

Richard LaLonde 5/18/86

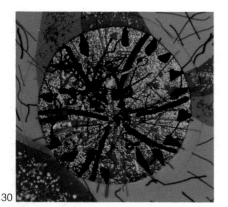

30

32

31

33

30. Richard LaLonde. *Detail: "Neptune's Waltz." Note small pieces of frit, confetti, and handmade stringer to achieve fine detail.*

31. Richard LaLonde. *Title: "Blast off to Oblivion;" 19" x 21" fused-glass panel with titanium frame and matte. Due to the lay-up process, titanium metal shows through the holes created in the piece.*

32. Richard LaLonde. *Title: "Neptune's Waltz;" 65" x 48", 1983, with Rick standing. This piece of fused glass is the beginning of the bringing to fruition his fantasy of architectural scale, illustrated in Figure 35.*

33. Richard LaLonde. *Detail: "Neptune's Waltz." This shows the torch-worked stringers and relief created by not firing to a full-flat fuse. This piece has textural as well as tactile qualities.*

36

34

35

Rick calls his work "futuristic nostalgia" – a vision of unseen worlds, undreamed concepts, and future possibilities – artwork one would see on a 23rd-century spacecraft.

"Happily, we unpacked our new cases of fusible Bullseye Glass and arranged them neatly by color. And we laughed, and we laughed, and we laughed, and said, "What a joy this fusing is! No more solder fumes in the face, no more putty under the fingernails, no more whiting in the hair."

34 and 36. Richard LaLonde. *Fused glass panels from titanium frame series; 19" x 21".*

35. Richard LaLonde. *Scale is fantasy, photographed with a magazine-paper cutout. Observing tiles in this fashion enables the artist's perceptions to be communicated.*

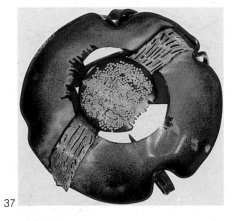

37

38

39

37. Charles Parriott. Slumped enamel bowl.

38. Charles Parriott. Sagged piece with a floating piece of mica; tips are fused to the bowl form.

39. Charles Parriott. Title: "Bombs Away," enameled and slumped; one of his fan series. The fan definition is formed by fusing on a fluted mold.

40. Charles Parriott. Social commentary piece; applied enamels using the sgraffito technique for the writing. The slumping and enamel-firing of the glass were performed in one process.

40

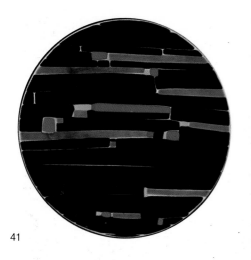

41

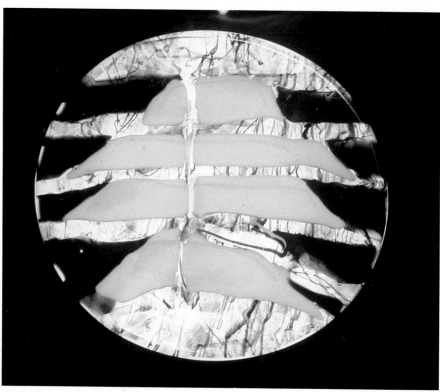

42

41. David Ruth. *14" fused glass plate; the clear base glass provides the light lines. The design is achieved by using dark colors directly over the clear glass.*

42. David Ruth. *10" bowl using combinations of Bullseye Glass and Uroboros stringer glass. We have found that many of Uroboros opals and stringer-confetti glasses are fusing compatible with Bullseye's glasses.*

43. David Ruth. *16" plate; part of a series using similar design elements. The use of a three-part design and a direct approach during the lay-up process create vitality and tension using simple strokes.*

44. David Ruth. *Title: "Orion I," 12½" diameter, fused glass sculpture. Piece achieves depth by using Bulleye #100 black over clear. The clear lines are as subtle as any lead lines, but these provide light transmission.*

43

44

45

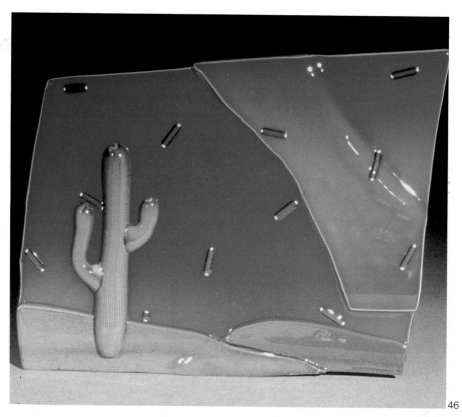

46

45. Kerry Feldman. *Cactus Series.*

46. Kerry Feldman. *Cactus series, 9" x 10", 1980. Using handmade flashed glass, relief is created by not fusing to fully flat.*

47. Kerry Feldman. *Cactus Series, 14" x 11", 1980. This piece was produced using the artist's own glass.*

48. Kerry Feldman. *Cactus series, 10" x 12", 1980. The rainbow over the cactus was created during the manufacturing of the glass. The cactus was hot-formed on a punty rod and later fused into panels.*

"The basic themes of my work in fused glass have been landscapes and windows. By using forms and color to develop ground and horizon, the resulting compositions refer to specific places either literally or abstractly. The use of a window is to indicate or suggest the different ways in which we observe things around us and to filter through the images we prefer."

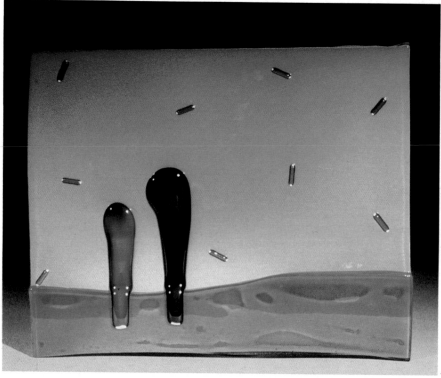

47

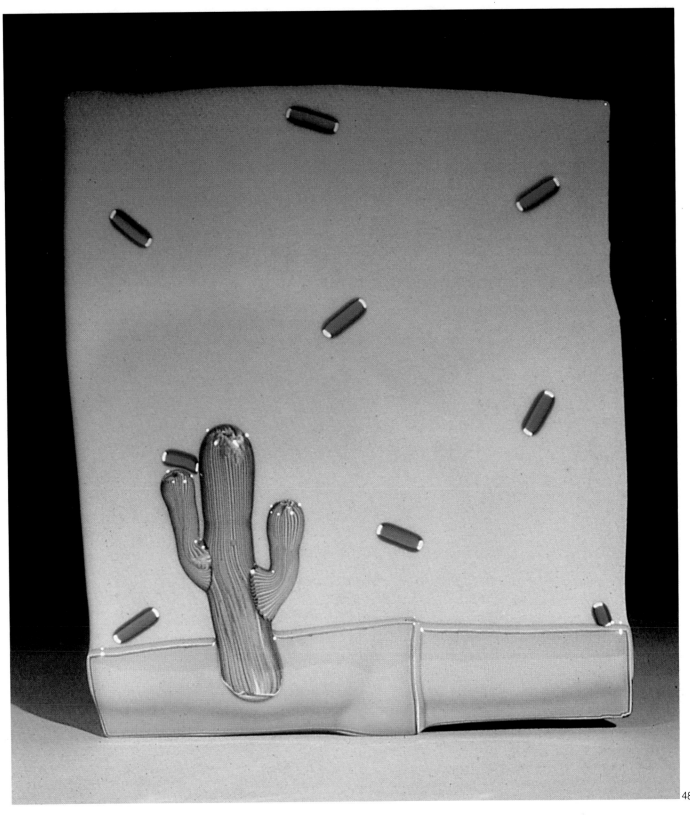

48

49

50

49. Ruth Brockmann. *Fused mask using Bullseye gold pink cathedrals and gold pink opalescents; torch-worked details. Note the use of transparent with opalescent glasses (the hair).*

50. Ruth Brockmann. *Fused mask using iridescent Bullseye glass, overlaid with clear glass and small pieces of frit, giving the mask a very hard, metallic appearance. Hair detail is made from iridescent gold pinks and #1108 marine blue cathedral.*

51. Ruth Brockmann. *Fused mask, life-size. The mustache is white overlay on black, and the beard is black overlay on white.*

52. Ruth Brockmann. *Fused mask using Bullrods for hair design. The piece was overglazed with metallic gold during the slumping process.*

53. Ruth Brockmann. *Brightly colored mask made with Bullseye opalescent glasses.*

51

52

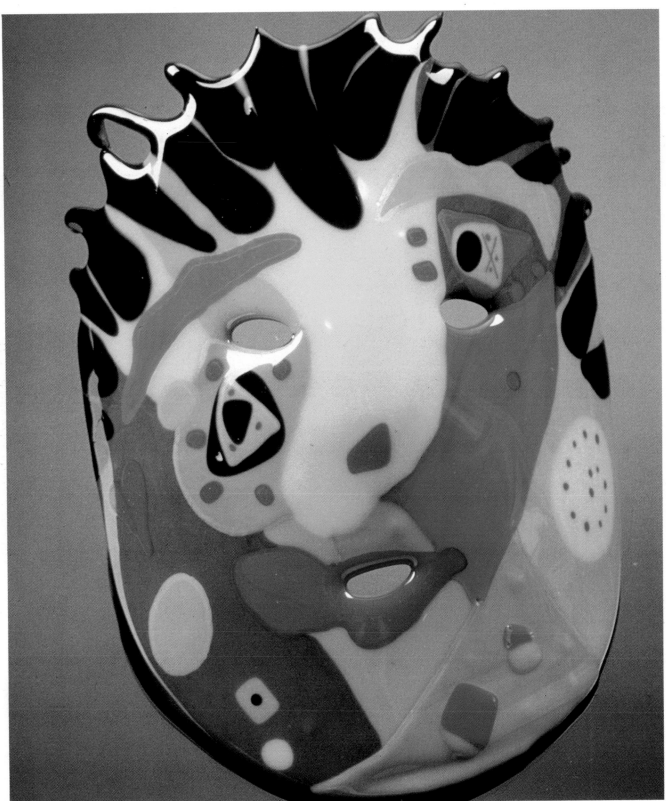

53

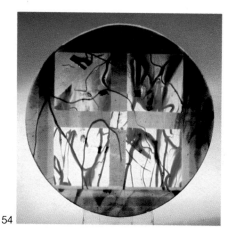

54

55

54. Jim Bowman. *14" plate. One of the first in a series of loose works using the glass surface to provide color in a painterly way. Clear glass adds depth in the same way varnish does in painting.*

55. Jim Bowman. *Three bowls with sandblasted lips and handles. The same process was used as in Figure 56.*

56. Jim Bowman. *Slumped bowl with sandblasted edge. This bowl was slumped through a ring mold and allowed to sag until the bottom flattened on the shelf. The lip has been sandblasted to create a soft transition.*

57. Jim Bowman. *"Self Portrait," 20" x 15". This piece was constructed of 3 separate tiles. The plaid shirt was created by using copper wire and copper foil tape between layers of Bullseye clear. Small pieces were used for the face and hair detail to achieve the painterly quality.*

"My first couple of years in glass were spent working with traditional stained/leaded techniques. As a painter, I felt all the normal frustrations of enclosed tight designs; fusing has allowed me to break out of those boundaries. I have been able to use all the elements of line, shape, color, and texture much more freely. I can see so many directions that fusing can be taken that I have to pull the reins in on myself in order to focus on an area for my work."

56

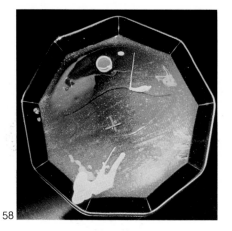

58

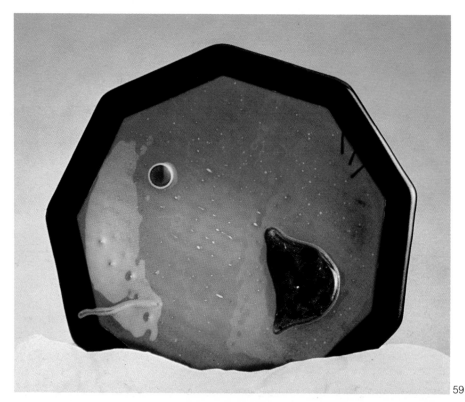

59

58. Gil Reynolds. *"Ganymede," 12"
diameter, polygon bowl, 1981. The lens
effect is used in this piece as it was in
Figure 59. Note that the volume of the
glasses was controlled sufficiently so
that all shapes making up the polygon
are outlined by the base glass.*

59. Gil Reynolds. *Title: "Near the Crowd,"
12" polygon bowl. Due to the hot working,
the previously torch-worked glass and
the pre-fused piece give this bowl a
loose quality, contrasting with the very
controlled outer shape.*

"My works are about an artist and his
creations existing in intellectual and spatial voids. I present my ideas in a nine-
sided, non-functional form that was derived from a combination of octagonal
oriental plates and traditional bowl
forms. I deal primarily with organic and
geometric objects suspended in various
spatial levels. These creations arise from
preconceived ideas that rely heavily
upon the opposition of contrasting
elements."

60. Gil Reynolds. *Title: "Hydra - The Play,"
octagon bowl with flame-worked overlays. Small circular dot in piece is 4
layers thick creating raised lens effect. In
this lens, the viewer can observe himself
looking at the piece of glass.*

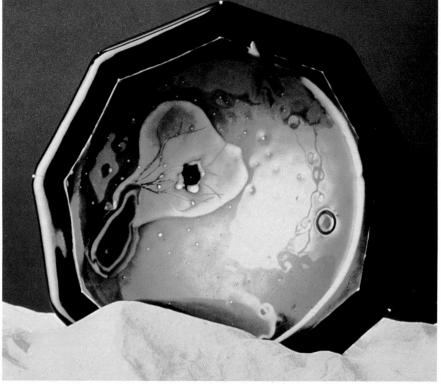

60

63

64

61

62

61. Mike Barton. *Title: "Crested Pecker." Frit was used in the design to create the fine-line detail.*

62. Mike Barton. *Title: "Dodo Bird," 12" diameter. Note the use of streaky glass to achieve shading in the face and beak.*

63. Mike Barton. *Title: "Praying Mantis," 12" diameter. Fine detail is achieved by using stringers.*

64. Mike Barton. *Title: "Ryan," 12" plate. Shadows and depth are created by choosing the specific surface quality of streaked Bullseye #123. Frit is used for shadowing detail. There is no painting on this piece.*

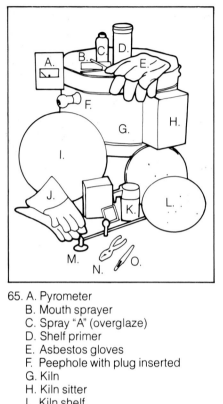

65. A. Pyrometer
    B. Mouth sprayer
    C. Spray "A" (overglaze)
    D. Shelf primer
    E. Asbestos gloves
    F. Peephole with plug inserted
    G. Kiln
    H. Kiln sitter
    I. Kiln shelf
    J. Terry cloth gloves
    K. Stressometer
    L. Slumping molds
    M. Circle cutter
    N. Grosing pliers
    O. Glass cutters

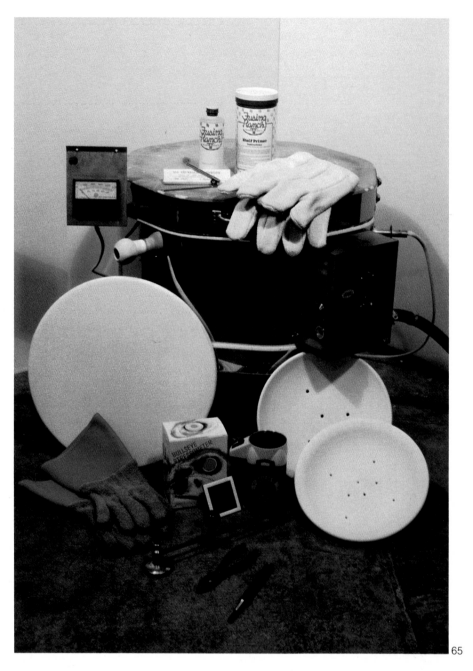

65

BASIC TOOLS AND SUPPLIES   CHAPTER 3

Today anyone can begin fusing glass by acquiring just a few essential pieces of equipment. With the availability of smaller, more efficient equipment, even the hobby craftsperson can now be equipped by investing several hundred dollars for the following four items: a kiln, a kiln shelf, shelf primer, and heat-protective gloves.

The kiln, or fusing oven, is the main piece of equipment necessary to fuse glass. This oven can be either salvaged from a past ceramic endeavor or newly purchased.

The difference between an oven constructed for ceramics or for glass fusing is the placement of the elements. A fusing kiln has the electrical elements in the top of the kiln; in the top-loader they are in the lid. The reason for this is to spread the heat evenly across the entire surface of the glass. A ceramic oven has its elements located around the inside perimeter of the walls. These two types of element configurations require different heating cycles and will be discussed in Chapter 10.

66

66. *Three types of surfaces on which to fuse: mullite clay, silicon carbide, and soft brick kiln shelves.*

The next necessary piece of equipment is the kiln shelf, upon which to assemble glass projects to be fused. The shelves, or fusing surfaces, can be made of various materials. Shelves made of clay (or mullite clay) and silicon carbide are most often used. The silicon carbide shelf has a tendency to lose its heat faster than mullite, allowing for a more even temperature distribution between the top and undersurface of the fused item. Despite this, we have not noticed any advantages over the clay shelf. In addition, the silicon carbide shelf has a rougher, more porous surface. High duty alumina casting bodies provide sizes not manufactured in regular clay shelves and also may be used for specific design requirements. The important aspect of any shelf is that it be flat and smooth, yet porous enough to accept the shelf primer that keeps the glass from sticking to the shelf.

A craftsperson working with large commercial pieces will use shelves of lightweight castables as well as marinite (a high duty insulation board) to suit his needs. The marinite may warp if not fired correctly, but both give up heat more slowly than would a dense material, which may cause warping of the fired glass and would become noticeable only after the glass has cooled completely. These materials also require a longer annealing cycle. (This is discussed further in Chapter 7.)

Another basic supply you will need is a good shelf primer, or kiln wash. This is necessary to keep the glass from sticking to the shelf at high temperatures. All separators work better at lower temperatures (below 1575 degrees F.); but at times it is very necessary to fire over this temperature (see "Basic Fusing Techniques," Chapter 6). In the case of combing, the temperature usually reaches 1650 to 1700 degrees F. At this temperature many separators fail and stick to the glass, causing an undesirable matte surface and a cleaning job you won't look forward to.

Currently on the market are Bullseye Shelf Primer, a specially designed kiln wash for glass, and Snyder's Separator. These products are made from basically the same materials as High Fire kiln wash used in cone 10 ceramics. The main ingredients are alumina hydrate 40-60% and pure kaolin clay (EPK) 60-40%. Calcium (whiting) in different molecular structures, carbon, and suspension agents such as gum or Bentonite can be added.

Bullseye Shelf Primer contains suspension agents (so mixing is quick and easy) that will not settle out of solution quickly. This aids in providing a uniform coating. The primer is color-coded for two reasons: 1) to be sure a fresh coat has been applied to the shelf (the blue-gray color burns out), and 2) to ensure the containers

67

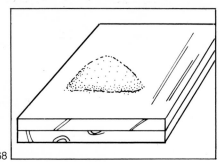

68

of mixed materials remain visually separate.

We firmly believe in applying all shelf primers wet and not powdering or sifting them onto the surface. Many dusting problems may occur, destroying the surface of a piece; our observations show better underside surfaces with use of a primer or separator applied as a wash.

Gloves are the fourth necessary item to set up your fusing workshop. Heat-protective gloves are absolutely essential. There is nothing more to say, except that without gloves, much of your fusing career will be spent with third-degree burns on your hands. From one point of view they may be your most cost-effective item.

Other Materials For Creative Exploration

In addition to the tools and supplies described above, there are several other materials that may be used to give creative dimension to your glass project. These include overglazes, sheet fiber paper, enamels, iridizing solutions, and lusters.

Overglazes

Overglazes are, by definition, composed of low melting glass (either lead or lead-free) ground to micron size. The agents for applying these glazes include thermoplastic squeegee oil, or spray media. The vehicle used will determine the workability and physical characteristics of the glaze prior to firing and will influence the fired results.

Several important factors to consider in the formulation of a glaze are the coefficient of expansion, maturing temperature, and chemical durability. Elements to consider in the choice of the vehicle are viscosity, drying time, adhesion, and dry strength. Common glazing agents include the use of sprays, squeegees, hand paints, decals, pad prints, and banding media.

There are some good reasons people use glazes on their glass projects. First, by using a glaze, you can eliminate the meticulous cleaning step required before firing. Second, the glaze eliminates devitrification and undesirable effects from fingerprints and glass cutting oil; it will also produce a higher gloss in those glasses which tend to fire to a dull surface. More important than using glazes as a means of eliminating the cleaning step (there is no substitute for proper technique) are the design possibilities that the selective, controlled use of glazes provides. For instance, when overglazes are applied to iridescent glass, the iridescent quality is lost. By masking off areas prior to applying the overglaze or by overlaying the iridescent areas with clear glass, the iridescent quality can be maintained and will remain a part of your design if you so desire. Color changes resulting from use of an overglaze containing lead is another area for design exploration. Lead especially affects selenium colors, turning reds to brown. This is generally undesired; however, it can be used as a technique to achieve design effects such as creating two colors from a single color, shading, or outlining.

Two very important factors are critical to the success of overglazing: glaze compatibility and proper application. Since overglazes become a thin layer of glass on the surface of the fused piece, its compatibility should be tested. This can be done by placing a ½"-diameter pile of the overglaze powder on two thicknesses of the clear base glass being used. Fire, using a normal fusing cycle, and check for stress by viewing the final piece with the Stressometer as outlined in Chapter 5 (or by other methods of determining stress and compatibility). Incompatibility will be evidenced by surface crazing or chipping off of the thin overglaze surface. These

67. Asbestos gloves, Spray "A," shelf primer, mouth sprayer, terry cloth gloves.

68. For testing overglazes, place a 1/2"-diameter pile of overglaze on two blanks of clear base glass. Fire, using normal fusing cycle.

70

69

may or may not be desired effects.

Proper application is another area of importance when applying overglaze. Disappointing results may occur if proper technique is not followed. Overglazes are available in either a dry powder form or a spray. Generally the spray is more easily applied. Spraying is an art within itself—but the technique is no different than spraying paint or lacquer. It is important to coat the edges of the glass; however, excessive spraying of the outside edges (which rest on the kiln shelf) should be avoided. Best results are obtained by aiming the nozzle at a right angle to the piece and at a distance of 6-10 inches. While proper application cannot be over-emphasized, several other factors need to be considered. Too generous an application may cause a blotchy, dull surface, while too sparing an application will not yield the desired results.

Because of the many variables inherent in formulating glazes (especially for use by diverse groups or in class situations), Bullseye Fusing Ranch has developed a glaze called Spray "A." It comes ready for use with any type of sprayer, dries quickly, and has sufficient dry strength so that pieces can be handled for careful re-assembly on the shelf. This enables one to selectively spray pieces and allows more latitude as a design technique.

69. Spraying surfaces of a piece with Spray "A."

70. Close-up showing an even coating of overglaze.

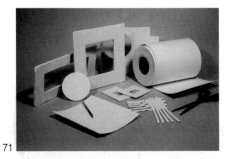

71

72

72a

71. *A 12" roll of 1/8" fiber paper shown with a variety of shapes on which to slump or sag glass.*

72. *Belt buckles fused over fiber cut-outs create a dimensional back that fits the bezel on the backside of the buckle.*

72a. *Belt buckles with belts.*

73. Liz Mapelli. *Tiles are fused onto fiber paper with the design side down. This provides a texture that reflects the iridescent qualities of the glass.*

74. Frances Higgins. *Enameled panel from one of two church windows. The outline of the hair was drawn with a stylus on a sheet of fired overall green, then filled in with enamel applied with a brush. The hair and background grain were drawn with another stylus.*

73

Sheet Fiber Paper

Sheet fiber paper, sometimes referred to as "fiberfrax" paper, may be used in a variety of ways to add creative dimension to your work. It is often cut into strips or shapes to give relief to the piece. The process consists of fusing the piece upside down (i.e., the desired surface is laid on the bottom side, next to the kiln shelf). Generally, this relief method, when used with thinner pieces of fiber paper, will leave a prominent texture on the bottom side of the glass piece . . . even more so than well-applied shelf primer. This is desirable if the fused pieces are going to be grouted or glazed to another surface (e.g., making tiles). It can also be used strictly as a separation between the kiln shelf and the object being fused (instead of kiln wash or shelf primer). It provides an excellent non-skid surface for floor tile.

In Figure 72 (the belt buckle project), sheet fiber paper was used to create a beveled (rabbet) back. This glass shape then fits into the bezel of the brass belt buckle. By using this process, you can create both a very strong glue joint for the buckle and a very nice finish.

Fiber paper and fiberboard are made of very fine alumina-silica threads in much the same way fiber glass is made. In the forming process, an organic binder is added to make the fiber stick together before it is rolled out into various thicknesses. Although this binder is not harmful (in fact, it is made from a sugar compound), your studio should be ventilated when firing fiber paper for the first time.

The binder must be fired out before the material is used next to the glass. To accomplish this, place pre-cut fiber pieces in a kiln and heat above 1200 degrees F. The fiber turns black when heated, and an acrid smoke is generated. After the binder has burned off, the paper will return to its original white surface.

Fiber paper has a tendency to stick to some colors of glasses more than others. In cases when fiber does stick, a wire brush is necessary to remove fiber residue.

74

75

76

Enamels

In the past, enamels were used for colorants on clear glass to avoid the compatibility problems in fusing together glasses of different colors. Enamels are usually added to a glass blank for color and textural reasons. Most enamels have been developed for decorating copper or other metal surfaces, but some enamels are made specifically for glass. Thompson has recently marketed Ice Fire enamels with expansion rates similar to those of float glass.

To achieve a brilliant color, many enamels are mixed with a high fluxing agent such as lead; these have a very high coefficient of expansion. Enamels will adhere to glasses as soon as the viscous range of the base glass has been reached (e.g., 1/8″ window glass softens at approximately 1300 degrees F.). However, when these highly fluxed enamels adhere to the sheet glass, the expansion rate is so different that the enamels tend to craze or spall off of the surface. High expansion enamels, therefore, are best suited for high expansion glasses or safer if sandwiched (and restrained) between two pieces of glass. The enamels, if less compatible, may be kept to a thinner layer which will not so greatly endanger the main glass body.

The extremely sparing application of enamel glass (in relation to the thickness of the parent glass to which it is being added) is the primary reason for success. For consistent results, the expansion coefficient of enamel should be matched to that of the base glass.

75. Gil Reynolds. *From a series of enameled triangles using diamond-cut, pre-fused bar sections. By using light enamels over dark glass, the enamels add an extra depth and dimension.*

76. Michael Higgins. *Shallow bowl (24″ diameter) made with 2 clear blanks pre-fired with enamels: one "winegold" luster enamel, the other white enamel. Pre-fired strips of various enameled colors were placed on top of the white enameled blank, enameled side up. The "winegold" enameled blank was then placed on the strips, enameled side down. It was then fused together. Trapped air bubbles create the subtle variation of colors and the halo effect.*

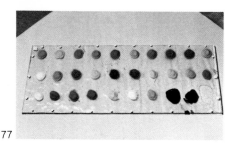

77

77. *When testing enamels for fusing compatibility with the base glass, place 1/8 tsp. of each ratio mix of enamel on the clear base glass to be tested. Fire to full fuse until mounds flatten.*

How to Get Enamel to Match the Coefficient of Expansion of Your Base Glass

The following is a method for mixing Thompson Enamel's Ice Fire and Lead Bearing Colors to match the coefficient of expansion of any base glass. Thompson Ice Fire Colors are compatible with float plate glass which has a coefficient lower than that of most stained glasses. The Lead Bearing Colors were designed to be fused to metal and have a coefficient which is much higher than that of most stained glasses.

To find the ratio of Ice Fire Colors to Lead Bearing Colors, place 1 tsp. of an Ice Fire Color (blue, for example) in a mortar. Add 1/8 tsp. of Lead Bearing blue, and mix with pestle. Remove 1/8 tsp. of the mixture and place in a mound on a labeled piece of clear test glass. This will equal an 8-1 ratio.

Add another 1/8 tsp. of Lead Bearing Color blue to the mixture already in the mortar; mix, and place 1/8 tsp. of the mixture on the same piece of labeled clear test glass (Figure 68). In a similar manner, mix ratios from 8-1 through 4-5; then fire all tests to full fuse until the mounds flatten. Let cool and read with a Stressometer. You should find that each color will have an optimum mixing ratio with any base glass you have tested.

To fit this blue enamel to Bullseye glasses, you might mix Ice Fire to Lead Bearing Colors in a 5-4 ratio. Yet, to fit black enamel to Bullseye, you might need a 7-2 mixing ratio. These ratios would be different for glasses of other manufacturers. Once you have tested several colors and found the correct mixing ratio for each, you will have a palette of enamels which is compatible with your current palette of fusible glasses.

Enamels mature at a temperature of 1250 to 1350 degrees F. (or when the entire surface has a glassy, wet appearance). We have fired most of our projects to higher temperatures (1475 to 1650 degrees F.) without any ill effects; however, the colors tend to dilute in intensity. At the Fusing Ranch, we use enamels for surface decoration, not sandwiched between layers of clear glass. The higher full-fuse temperature causes many enamels to give up oxygen (causing bubbles) at approximately 1500 degrees F.

Best results will be obtained with high contrasting glass-enamel combinations (e.g., black glass with white enamel). Although low contrast combinations will work, they require a larger amount of enamel than do high contrast combinations. (See 'Glassery' for Thompson enamels.)

Enamels may be applied to base glass by dusting, sprinkling, spattering, trailing with a syringe (or stylus), stenciling, silk-screening, or detailing with an air brush (and other traditional brushing techniques). These techniques are explained in many books available on enameling. Frances Higgins uses a stylus technique which she developed after many years of experimentation. Frances works a glass tube (1/4-3/8") in a flame, slowly drawing the tube apart making the mid-section smaller. Control of this process requires practice. The glass tube is broken in the middle, making two eyedropper-shaped tubes. The small end is ground or sanded flat, and a rubber bulb with a small hose is attached to the opposite end. By holding a finger over the hole in the bulb, properly ground and strained enamels can be drawn into the stylus. When air is allowed to enter the bulb, the enamel will flow at a constant rate, controlled by the viscosity of the liquid enamel and the size of the small eyedropper opening. This technique allows great control and artistic freedom in the application of enamel.

Michael and Frances Higgins have been working with enamels on window glass since 1942. Through various business ventures and a great deal of experimentation, they have established a palette of enamels on glass with colors ranging from primary to tertiary. The enamels the Higgins use were developed for the type of window glass which was sold 30 years ago. For the past 20 years, window glass has been manufactured using the float process. (See 'Glassery' for definition.) Although today's glass differs in expansion from that in use by the Higgins, the enamel processes they have developed can be applied to today's float glass with slight modifications. In "Glass Fusing, Book Two" (the advanced edition), we hope to share the wealth of Michael's experience through reprints of published articles.

The most important thing to understand, before learning technique, is how to test the available enamel combinations. Enamels can be used in conjunction with overglazes, lusters, chunks of frit, glass beads, millefiore glass, etc. Enamel should be ground with a mortar and pestle and extended with an overglaze medium to be painted onto a piece of glass. An even thickness of the enamels will diminish the chances of chipping off or cracking caused by uneven stresses.

Cutting Glass

Many books have been written on the various techniques of cutting glass. Certainly, all have their individual merits. This discussion of glass cutting will apply directly to the cutting of glass for fusing only.

Generally speaking, glass cutting for fusing does not require the accuracy necessary with other methods of fitting pieces together. A glass fuser can choose to work in a loose mode with found pieces, scraps, and broken or smashed chips. By using a glass cutter, having only the most rudimentary skills, intricate and amazing pieces can be created. The ability to cut strips I/2 to ⅜"-inch wide (either freehand or by using a straightedge or strip cutter) is sufficient to create the pieces illustrated.

An interesting design can be achieved by first cutting two pieces of glass to approximately the same size. Using one piece, place it between a few folds of newspaper and strike it with a heavy object. (We like to use a rock for this purpose.) By carefully opening the paper without disturbing the separate pieces, this fractured design can be arranged individually on the first blank and fused into one piece. Experimenting with the shape of struck objects and/or pre-scoring the blank to be struck adds many interesting possibilities for design.

The mosaic technique of assembling small pieces on top of one solid blank is another way to achieve great image capacity without having to cut glass accurately. On the other hand, if matching individual pieces are prepared by cross-hatching with a glass cutter, strip-cutting the design becomes very much like tile lay-up.

78

Cutting Already Fused Pieces

Solid full-fused pieces will sometimes break or have a small defect. If the break is caused by a foreign material in the glass such as a stone (see 'Glassery' for definition), the small object can be cut out and the piece can be fused again. On the other hand, if you simply do not like the piece but would like to use a part of it in another piece, you're in luck. Score the fused piece with a glass cutter and hold it firmly. The fused glass will break just as would any other glass 1/4 inch thick or thicker. To better understand what cutting fused glass would be like, practice on 1/4 inch clear plate glass.

Glass that has not been fully fused (the surface is irregular) may break erratically and will follow the path of least resistance. In a case such as this, a diamond band saw or diamond cut-off saw should be used.

We have found that broken fused glass pieces and/or mistakes become meaningful with time. As long as the glass is compatible with the existing palette in the studio, everything should be saved. Cross sections of pre-fused glass are inspiring, and many techniques rely upon using pre-fused pieces that have been diamond cut, strip cut, or simply broken.

78. Dale Busaker. *Plates and bowls using simple strip-cutting techniques (see Chapter 8).*

79. Liz Mapelli. *Fused platter using simple glass-cutting techniques to create a complex piece.*

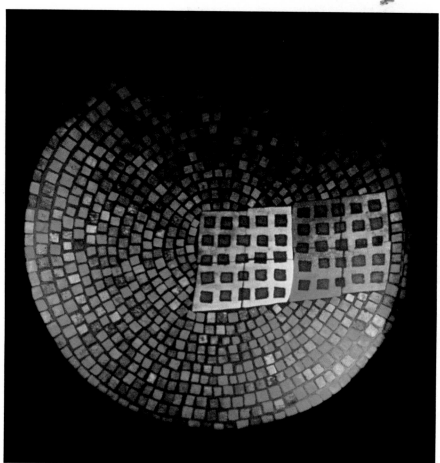

79

PREPARING FOR FIRING CHAPTER 4

Preparing for your first glass fusing project, however small or large, will take much careful preparation. The recommendations we have outlined in this chapter are starting points based on our experiences both at our facility and at workshops around the country. These recommendations will assist in producing successful results.

Kiln Preparation

Check your kiln lid to see that it fits tightly and that hinges fit properly. If not, cut a ceramic fiber gasket to fill the void. It is necessary to know where heat is escaping from the kiln so it can be controlled.

If your kiln has a peephole, be sure the plug fits tightly and is in good condition. You will be removing and replacing the plug often to inspect the piece inside, and if it is unbroken and fits properly, you will avoid burning yourself. Kilns equipped with automatic shut-offs (e.g., timers or kiln sitters) should be checked and adjusted according to manufacturer's instructions. In the case of the Bullseye/Octagon, refer to the Firing Schedule for use with the kiln sitter.

The kilns discussed in this book have been designed for safe home use. The outside skin temperature will not exceed 200 degrees F.; however, standard precautions dictate setting your kiln no closer than 18″ to any flammable material.

Know Your Pyrometer

When preparing your kiln for fusing, don't forget one of the most important pieces of equipment—the pyrometer.

The pyrometer should be mounted firmly in a vertical position and placed where it will not be bumped. Most pyrometers are meant to be used with a specific thermocouple and a specific lead wire length. If these are not matched, the temperature readings will be inaccurate. Remember, the red and black leads may not be interchanged. Black is always positive (+).

At Bullseye Glass, we have developed a method of setting the pyrometer (this is done with a small set screw on the face) using a small cone 019. Cone 019 will bend at 1333 degrees F. according to the Orton Manufacturing Co. The reason for using a cone 019 as a set point is that it is midway between fusing and annealing temperatures. By adjusting your pyrometer with a ceramic cone in the following way, all the temperatures in this book should be accurate enough for successful work.

Place a small cone 019 in a clay wad so it will stand at a slight angle. With a sharp pencil, poke holes in the wet clay to avoid shattering when heating rapidly, or prepare well ahead of time and let the clay dry thoroughly. When firing a piece in your kiln, place the upright cone in front of the peephole on the shelf with your fused piece. When the cone bends, but before it is flat, adjust your pyrometer temperature indicator needle by turning the set screw on the front to indicate 1333 degrees F. All but the most expensive pyrometers have marks only every 25 degrees F., so you will have to estimate the needle location for this specific temperature.

80. First insert a 019 cone into a wad of wet clay at a slight angle, poking holes in the clay so it won't shatter during firing. Place the cone in front of the peephole.

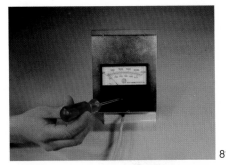

81. When the cone bends, adjust the pyrometer set screw to read 1333 degrees F.

4

82. Tools and supplies used to prepare a kiln shelf. From top (clockwise): bench brush, shelf primer, container with pre-mixed shelf primer and application brush, spatula, fabri-cut.

83. Removing shelf primer with spatula from previously used kiln shelf.

Shelf Preparation

The quality of the shelf primer, the care of application, and the texture of the kiln shelf or other fusing surface are the three elements that will affect the underside surface of your fused piece.

Shelf primer, separator, or kiln wash are all high-temperature clay and alumina mixtures. The fine particles of clay in most mixes help to keep the hydrated alumina in suspension and allow a smooth application. Most commercial high-fire kiln wash mixes found in ceramic stores will work and will keep the glass from adhering to the shelf surface. Bullseye Shelf Primer is a specially formulated mix containing suspension agents that, when applied according to directions, generally works better than other commercial mixes.

If no separator is applied to a shelf (or mold), the glass will stick to the shelf and will crack upon cooling. This is because glass shrinks more than the clay or other material from which the shelf is made.

Some properties of Shelf Primer are lost after a high temperature firing and, for this reason, a new coat should be applied after each firing. When using Shelf Primer over a slumping form or mold, it is not necessary to remove the primer or to apply a fresh coat before slumping a second time with the same mold. This is because slump temperatures are reached at approximately 1200 to 1300 degrees F. and the separator has not been changed enough to lose its release properties.

The most important step in using any shelf primer or release is the application process. This powdered material should be added to 5 parts water by volume, then mixed thoroughly. The solution will appear watery and if allowed to sit for very long will separate, becoming thicker on the bottom of the container. Always mix well before using each time.

Any type of brush or spray gun may be used to apply the primer. In the case of brushes (which we prefer), a soft, natural bristle brush approximately 3" wide works well. We recommend using a 3" Chinese haik brush. Nylon brushes used for applying latex paint are also acceptable, but they are not as fine bristled and will leave larger ridges in the final coat. This is fine if you desire this particular effect on your fused glass piece.

After starting with a clean shelf (one that has had all the old primer removed with a spatula or putty knife and sanded), apply the first coat of primer liberally, stroking in one direction. Because the solution is thin, you will be able to see the brush marks. Immediately reload the brush with more primer and apply a second coat at a right angle to the first coat. The shelf will appear a little darker and its surface will be thoroughly soaked with water. One more coat may be applied instantly. The third coat should be applied, as before, at a right angle to the previous one.

At this time the shelf will look wet and will show white or gray streaks from the bristle pattern in the brush (that's good). As the shelf dries, the surface will become chalky, and you will no longer be able to see the surface of the original shelf material.

The shelf may be dried in the kiln, in your studio, or in the sun. Speed of drying does not affect the performance of the shelf separator. We usually turn our fusing kiln to medium heat and set one or two shelves on the edge, drying the shelf from the bottom side and driving the water out.

84. *Sanding the kiln shelf with fabri-cut assures a clean surface for a fresh application of shelf primer. After sanding, the shelf should be cleaned with a bench brush.*

85. *The first coat of shelf primer is applied with slow, even, and continuous strokes in one direction.*

86. *The second coat of shelf primer is immediately applied at a right angle to the first coat.*

87. *The final coat of shelf primer is immediately applied at a right angle to the previous coat.*

Shelves dried from the top (or out in the sun) sometimes fool you because only the surface dries. Moisture can then cause problems if trapped under the glass. You are assured of eliminating all moisture in the shelf if it is dried from the bottom up.

The resulting thin, but even, primer coat is ready for stacking glass; however, if an even smoother surface is desired, rub your hand lightly across it. This will raise a very thin powder on the surface, and any brush marks or ridges remaining from application will be removed.

Another method of application is powdering the surface of a dry shelf with a separator using 120 mesh (or finer) sifting screen, but we find this method inferior to liquid application.

Spraying the primer on is an adequate method, but it is more difficult to tell when the proper amount of wash has been applied; also the wash or primer has a tendency to ball up in the air when sprayed, causing a spackled texture on the shelf.

The most often observed defects found when watching students prepare shelves are: 1) the wash has been applied too thickly (because of inadequate water addition); 2) not all of the previous wash was removed from the shelf and much more primer adhered where old primer remained, leaving an uneven surface; and 3) the student was sloppy, leaving gobs of primer sticking to the edges of the shelf; when the shelf is handled, primer falls onto other completed and cleaned work.

Shelf primer is a refractory material, which if dripped or powdered onto the surface of a glass piece before firing, will leave a defect. Keep the edges of the shelves clean when firing the *Octagon*, where two shelves are often fired one over the other. When the top shelf is set in place, kiln wash may fall on projects below.

There is no primer or other fusing surface which allows the bottom of a piece to come out as smoothly as the top. Other methods (e.g., diamond-ground shelves, meticulous application, sanding primer, or carbon produced from torch application) have all been tried, but to our knowledge, none have worked better than the simple, hand-rubbed application of Shelf Primer.

88

89

Questions Commonly Asked About Kiln Preparation

"Must the old primer be sanded off completely? Can't I simply add another coat?"

Although this will sometimes work, you take the chance of ruining the whole project.At times when we are in a hurry and firing only test bars, we will lightly sand the shelf surface before applying a fresh coat of primer. Since Bullseye Shelf Primer is color-coded (i.e., the mix contains a dye that fires out at 1000 degrees F.), we can usually be assured of covering the entire shelf.We know the primer is fresh if the shelf has an even, liquid, blue-gray surface.

"Sometimes I'm in a hurry.Is it necessary to thoroughly dry the shelf primer?"

Nearly every time the shelf primer is not allowed to dry thoroughly, something will go wrong: either bubbling, sticking, or cracking will occur. We did, however, discover one production method that was successful. After the shelf had been prepared and was still wet, four very small pieces of glass (the size of match heads) were placed on the shelf. The glass assembly to be fused was then placed on these small glass cullet pieces. Because the kiln was brought up to temperature slowly with the lid cracked, the shelf was allowed to dry before the blank sagged over the cullet. In this case, production light fixtures were being made using all cathedral glasses. The small stilt pieces of cullet were the the same color as the base blank and, therefore, could not be detected in the finished piece.

"What can I do to protect the floor of my kiln from the effects of overfiring?"

It is always a good idea to paint the bottom of your kiln with a heavy coat of shelf primer before firing in case any glass runs off the shelf or melts onto the bottom in the event of a blow-up. Hot glass next to insulation brick will eat into the brick; when the glass is chipped out, it will leave a pit or pockmark. In time, your kiln may lose efficiency. In the case of fiber-insulated kilns, the shelf primer or kiln wash should not be used. Instead, a coating cement used in making fiber molds should be applied.This will harden the surface and make it resistant to deterioration caused by glass eating into the fiber.

"Shelf primer is generally applied sparingly. By varying this, can I use shelf primer as a design element?"

Yes.Some artists apply shelf primer very, very generously and then create patterns in the wet primer.This will give a heavy or patterned surface to the underside of the glass.

For this purpose, shelf primer is added to approximately one part water (to the consistency of cake frosting) and then applied in lines and spots using a cake decorator to create relief up to 1/4 inch high. This mixture should dry thoroughly before setting glass over it, otherwise bubbles will be created from the water vapor. When using cathedral and clear glasses, many wonderful patterns can be achieved with this method. The primer will crack and will show small stretch marks after drying fully, but these do not usually affect the final design. Remember to apply primer to the entire shelf before overapplying the heavy primer mix for texture.

88. D. Wright. *Wall hanging using thick shelf primer that has been squeezed from a cake decorator for a textural effect. The primer must be allowed to dry thoroughly before placing glass on top.*

89. *Detail of textures formed by thick shelf primer.*

COMPATIBILITY AND TESTING CHAPTER 5

Compatibility and Testing

Assembling a compatible palette of colored glasses is the aim of any glass artisan who hopes to expand his own creative horizons in fused glass. Having a compatible palette of colored glasses requires careful record-keeping and a clear understanding of a few basic concepts . . . most importantly, the understanding of and testing for glass compatibility.

Colored glass formulas and procedures used by the various glass manufacturers vary greatly. As a result, the glasses of one manufacturer are usually not compatible with those of another. Therefore, we suggest selecting all glasses from the same manufacturer even though all colored glasses may be neither compatible with each other nor may their compatibility be necessarily consistent from one batch to another. Bullseye has, however, developed a line of compatible colored glasses labeled "tested compatible." The experience gained in developing a means of testing for fusing compatibility is the basis of this chapter. By knowing the procedures outlined, a compatible palette of glasses may be readily assembled.

Compatibility

In the world of glass fusing, two glasses are compatible if they can be fused together and, after proper cooling to room temperature, have no undue stresses in the finished piece that will lead to fracturing.

It is important to define compatibility within the framework of the craft of glass fusing. The craftsperson is interested in fusing colored glasses to produce an object that will not crack under normal conditions. These conditions may require withstanding temperature extremes (from repeated cycles through a dishwasher to the climate-controlled environment of a gallery). Whatever the destination of the fused glass piece, the compatibility of the various glasses used will play a major role in its survival.

Glass, like most materials, expands when heated and contracts when cooled. If two glasses that do not expand or contract similarly are fused together, unwanted stresses will develop in the glass. (See diagram illustrating compatibility stresses on page 44.)

The greater the difference in contraction or expansion of the fused glasses, the greater these stresses become. If these stresses are extreme, the two pieces will break apart upon cooling. If these stresses are moderate, the pieces will remain together upon cooling but will not endure sudden temperature changes such as those experienced in a dishwasher cycle. Compatibility stresses, whether great or small, cannot be eliminated by annealing.

Cracking due to incompatibility can be readily distinguished from cracking due to improper annealing. By examining the cracked piece, it will be noted that incompatibility fractures will follow the interfaces of the colored glasses. In contrast, fractures will randomly cross color boundaries if glasses that are compatible have been improperly annealed.

90

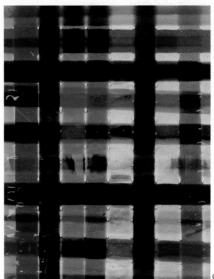

91

90. Fused glasses which are incompatible exhibit fractures and numerous areas of stress due to differences in expansion and contraction upon heating and cooling.

91. Fused glasses which are compatible will exhibit very little stress due to similar coefficients of expansion. If the expansion coefficients of fused glasses are in a range of plus or minus 1 of one another, they will be fusing compatible.

Coefficients of Expansion

Generally, two different colored glasses are compatible with each other if they both expand and contract similarly when heated or cooled. This is stated by saying that two glasses have a similar coefficient of expansion.

The coefficient of expansion is a number that expresses a percentage change in length, per degree change in temperature. The coefficient of expansion is determined by measuring the change in length of glass for a one-degree Centigrade increase in temperature. It is obviously a very small number (Bullseye glass is 0.0000090). For simplicity's sake when comparing expansion coefficients of different glasses, all the zeros are ignored; thus, Bullseye glass would have a coefficient of 90. (See "Chart of Expansion Coefficients of Some Common Glasses" on page 44.)

The range of fusing compatibility is plus or minus 1. Therefore, Bullseye #101F with a coefficient of 90 would be fusing compatible with other glasses whose coefficients range from 89 to 91. Outside this range, undue stresses will develop in the glass. When two glasses whose coefficient numbers differ by more than 5 are fused together, the internal stress developed in the glass is tremendous . . . high enough to exceed the tensile strength of glass and to cause failure by cracking.

Coefficient of expansion numbers should be regarded as starting points from which to experiment rather than definitive numbers not to be questioned. Laboratory tests used to determine the coefficients of expansion are performed in the temperature range of 0 to 300 degrees C. (32 to 512 degrees F.). Glasses usually exhibit a fairly constant expansion rate through this temperature range. However, in fusing two different glasses together, the expansion from 300 degrees upward through the strain point (which may vary markedly) is as important as expansion in the lower range.

This explains why some glasses that have the same coefficient number, as determined by a laboratory, do not always fit each other when fused together. A reliable test for a good expansion fit between two glasses is to fuse the two together and test the resultant piece for stress. We recommend the Stressometer test method. This is explained in detail later in this chapter under "Methods of Testing."

One additional physical property of glasses involved in fusing compatibility is the fiber softening point. The fiber softening point determines the annealing range, and therefore the strain point, for a particular glass. (See detailed definitions in the 'Glassery' and in Chapter 7.)

The magnitude of the expansion coefficient number is a relative measure of how much a particular glass expands upon heating. The larger the number, the greater the expansion. Lower coefficients have better resistance to thermal shock. A Pyrex glass with a coefficient number of 32 can withstand great thermal shock (e.g., glass flameware).Bullseye at 90 can withstand repeated cycles in a dishwasher. Glasses with expansion coefficients over 100 usually break during the first cycle in a dishwasher. Therefore, it is useful to know the expansion coefficients of the glasses with which you are working for both compatibility and application.

Testing for Compatibility

Care in testing procedure and record-keeping is essential to obtain consistent and accurate test results. Both the sample glass and the sheet of glass from which the sample was taken must be labeled with the same number. This should always be done immediately to avoid error. We recommend an Alton steel marking pen for labeling the test samples. This marker writes in white, adheres well to the glass, and does not fire-off at full-fuse temperatures. Various methods are available for testing the compatibility of colored glasses. Three such methods include 1) the thread-pull test, 2) the Stressometer test, and 3) the bar test. These are described in detail in this section. We recommend the Stressometer test over all others; however, the thread-pull and bar tests provide useful information.

The thread pull test (illustrated in Figures 92 through 97) has the advantage of being performed very quickly and without the use of a kiln. However, this very advantage detracts from its relevance to compatibility. The test is based on the fact that if a thread is pulled from two glasses that do not contract similarly, the thread will be curved . . . the degree of curvature being a measure of incompatibility. Probably the most useful information the thread-pull test provides is indicating which of the two glasses has a higher expansion coefficient (the glass on the inside of the curve).

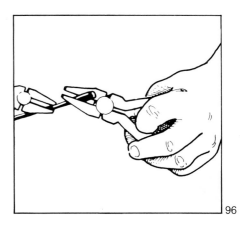
96

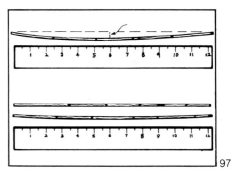
97

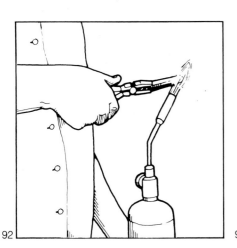
92

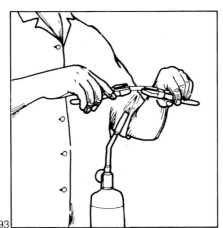
93

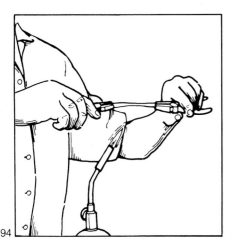
94

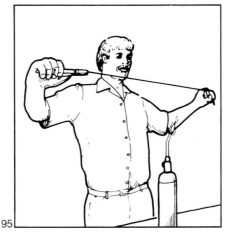
95

92. Cut a small piece from each of two different glasses. Each piece should be approximately 3/16" to 1/4" wide, and 3" long. Place the two pieces of glass together and grasp securely with pliers. Use a torch to heat them until they are tightly fused together. (Rotate pieces slowly until they become a dull red color and just before they start to run.)

93. Holding another pair of pliers in your other hand, attach them to the top of the fused glass.

94. Quickly pull the glass by stretching your arms apart as far as possible.

95. Hold this position until the glass "sets" or becomes brittle (occurs within a few seconds).

96. Break the two ends off with pliers. The glass strand should be at least 12 inches long.

97. If the piece remains straight, the glasses are compatible. If the piece curves more than 1/4" for every foot, the glasses have unequal coefficients of expansion and will not successfully fuse together.

98

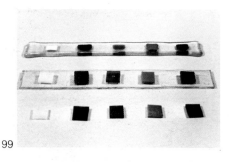

99

The results of the thread-pull test must be used with discretion for the following reason. Once the glasses are fused together in the flame of the torch, the thread is stretched and quickly cools to room temperature. This renders the test less reliable since it does not duplicate the actual cooling cycle the glasses would experience in the kiln during fusing. Only with experience can consistent threads be pulled. Care must be taken to prevent the thread from rotating when pulled; the thread must be held taut until the glass is rigid, otherwise the results will be incorrect.

The Stressometer test is a more foolproof method to determine compatible glass combinations. (The steps involved in this test are illustrated in Figures 98 through 100.) By using this method, any number of glasses may be tested at the same time. Since this test is performed under conditions identical to those used in producing the final fused glass piece, it is indeed a **TRUE** test. An added bonus of this test is that it will also indicate any color changes which may occur in the glass due to the heat treatment during fusing.

The one requirement is that all colored glasses must be tested against a clear base glass. All glasses used must be those of the same manufacturer . . . both the clear base glass and the colored glasses being tested. In the case of Bullseye glass, all #101F clear has been tested at the factory to assure a constant coefficient of 90. When using other manufacturer's clear glass as a base, reserving one or more sheets of the clear glass to be used only for ongoing testing is recommended.

After following the steps illustrated in Figures 98 through 100, the test strip is viewed on the Bullseye Stressometer as shown in Figure 101. The Bullseye Stressometer is a device designed to enable the glass artisan to visually detect stress in glass. This device can be used to detect stress due to the use of incompatible glasses as well as stress due to improper annealing. All glasses exhibiting slight or no stress are fusing compatible with each other. (See 'Glassery' for a detailed description of the Stressometer.)

98. Bullseye Stressometer.

99. Cut a strip of clear glass 1-1/2 inches in width and approximately 6 to 8 inches long. This is your BASE GLASS. All glasses which are compatible with the base clear glass will be compatible with each other. Cut a small square (1/2"x 1/2") of all glasses you wish to test. Place them one inch apart on the base clear glass and fuse them flat at 1500 to 1550 degrees F. Annealing for 15 minutes at 950 degrees F. is essential to achieve an accurate visual reading.

100. To observe stress, place the fused test strip over the lens of the Stressometer. Place the second lens (mounted in a slide holder) over the fused test strip and rotate slowly. When the maximum light blockage occurs, a halo or flare (much like a solar flare during a total eclipse) will appear if excess stress is present. The halo will not appear if stress does not exist. The initial fusing test will also show any color shift or color change which may occur when fusing.

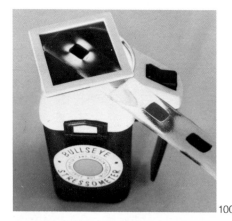

100

Chart of coefficient of some glasses

BULLSEYE 101 F		90
FLOAT PLATE	PPG	86
	GUARDIAN	85
SPECTRUM		94-98
BOTTLE GLASS		89-92
CORNING 7052		46
PYREX		32

101

| SLIGHT STRESS | LIGHT STRESS | MODERATE STRESS | HIGH STRESS | EXTREME STRESS |

The bar test is a good test for fusability because it, like the Stressometer test, is performed under conditions identical to those used in producing the finished pieces (i.e., on a kiln shelf in the same kiln using the same firing schedule, etc.). The bar test, however, enables one to determine which glass is expanding (or shrinking) more than the other. The Stressometer test indicates a stress between a colored glass and the base clear glass, whereas the bar test can be used to test one color against another color, at the same time indicating which one is shrinking more. However, the tolerances are much smaller on the bar test, and therefore require more precise measuring. Preferably, a micrometer should be used to measure the curvature.

To perform the bar test, cut 1"-wide, 12"-long strips of the two glasses to be tested. Lay one strip on top of the other and fuse flat in the kiln. Use the normal firing cycle for two layers of glass. (Proper annealing is always a requirement in compatibility testing.)

When the fused bar is at room temperature, lay it on a straightedge. If the fused bar is straight, the two glasses are compatible. If the bar bends, the amount of the bend is a measure of the degree of incompatibility. This curvature should be less than 3/32" over the 12" length.

Fusing two sets of bars at the same time is recommended . . . one set with glass #1 on top, and one with glass #2 on top. The reason for this is to eliminate possible inconsistencies in cooling caused by the kiln shelf. Since the bottom layer of glass cools through the kiln shelf and the top layer of glass cools through the air, a different cooling rate may occur between the top and the bottom. If this difference exists through the annealing range, the strip will have a permanent bend which will not be related to differences in coefficients. A control bar (such as two strips of the same glass fused together) can also be used to determine if there is a bending due to differential cooling. This in itself is a good test to run if warping is apparent in the finished fused glass pieces. If the center of the bar lifts up from the kiln shelf, it indicates that the shelf was hotter than the surrounding air in the kiln through the annealing zone. If the ends of the bar lift up from the shelf, the opposite is true. This problem should be alleviated by a slower cooling cycle through the anneal cool. After the fused bars have cooled, each one should be laid on a flat surface (such as a straightedge) and the curvature measured with a micrometer. The bar should not have a curvature greater than 3/32" over the 12" length to be fusing compatible.

Conclusion

The usefulness of any compatibility testing method depends upon how closely it duplicates the actual production conditions. The Stressometer test is the recommended test for the fuser. It is the easiest test to reproduce, it is performed using the identical process as that producing the final fused piece, and the results are easily interpreted. For the advanced artist, the Stressometer can be used in combination with the thread-pull or bar tests to give additional input. However, keep in mind that the thread-pull test requires more skill and experience, and it is not done in the kiln firing situation. For the bar test to yield useful information, an accurate measuring device such as a micrometer is needed.

102

103

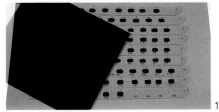

104

105

103. *Compatibility tests after fusing. The Stressometer test strips are ready for viewing. The bar tests are ready for measurements with a micrometer.*

104. *Viewing the Stressometer test strips on a light table with a large sheet of Polaroid™ film underneath, and a 12" square sheet of Polaroid film over the top.*

105. *Records are kept on all results.*

102. *Kiln shelf (20" x 20") with compatibility test prepared for fusing. Note that there are 6 bar tests and 9 Stressometer tests. On the Stressometer strips, a* triangular edge has been cut off. This is then laid on top of itself to check the quality of annealing in the test fusing cycle.

Temperature Chart

0-1000 degrees F.		All domestic colored, opal, and cathedral glasses remain rigid but are expanding at a rate determined by their coefficients of expansion. Uniform heating over the entire surface of the glass is important at these temperatures. All glasses will have reached their strain point and will no longer break from thermal shock. Added organic material (i.e., white glue, paper, fiber paper binding agents, squeegee oil, and other organics) volatilize, and the fumes dissipate. For this reason, the lid should be propped open ½ inch when organic material is present.
1000-1200 degrees F. *Cone 21 - 1189°F*		There is no visible change in double-strength float glass. Very thin confetti glass flattens and edges blunt. Most domestic glasses slump if the rise in temperature has been very slow. Above this temperature, fluorine opals increase in density (referred to as the striking range). Metallic lusters are mature. Iridizing solution may be sprayed on the glass surface.
1200-1300 degrees F.		All domestic and foreign glasses tested slump in this 100-degree range. The edges of the glass remain square or become slightly rounded.
1300-1350 degrees F. *Cone 19 1333°*		Many glasses devitrify if held too long between 1300 and 1450 degrees F. Bullseye glass has rounded edges and is fully slumped. Float glass has not fully slumped; edges are square.
1350-1400 degrees F.		Bullseye glass (if only one layer thick) is starting to contract. Surface tension is greater than the pull of gravity, making the glass pull in and rise up. Float glass is fully bent or sagged. Most enamels are mature at this temperature. Surfaces of glasses which are prone to devitrification become wrinkled.
1400-1450 degrees F. *Cone 17 1443°*		Two layers of Bullseye glass are fully laminated and stick together (referred to as the "fuse-to-stick" temperature) Double-strength window glass edges are fully rounded. This is a transitional temperature range for many glasses; visual perception of glass shows slow, but constant, movement. The surface of Bullseye is flowing and liquid at this temperature. Once this occurs, glass will no longer devitrify.
1450-1550 degrees F. *Cone 16 1517* *Cone 15 1549°*		Single-strength window glass is flowing and liquid as was Bullseye glass 100 degrees F. earlier; it will contract after forming needlepoints along the edges. Bullseye glass is flowing together. Gravity overtakes surface tension, and glass pieces flatten and enlarge if the glass volume is great enough. This is the range where many fusers choose to fuse soak (see "Techniques of Firing").
1550-1600 degrees F. *Cone 13 1615°*		Bullseye glass is flowing. The surface is flat. Small bubbles trapped between layers will rise to the surface but will not burst.
1600-1700 degrees F. *Cone 12 - 1650°* *Cone 11 - 1680°* *Cone 10 - 1686*		Bubbles will break through the surface of Bullseye glass. Different colors, whether cathedrals or opals, have slightly different surface tension characteristics; bubbles will burst at different times within this temperature range. Bullseye iridescent glasses have a very high surface tension. Glass viscosity and surface tension are low enough that the glass may be combed. (See Chapter 15.)

Annealing See page 53 Sect 7

Glass See - 9

Kilns See 10

BASIC FUSING TECHNIQUES 6

In this chapter we will examine some basic techniques used in fusing glass. These will include understanding the properties of glass during firing, achieving different colors when fusing two or more glasses together, controlling volume of one or more layers of glass, and examining several techniques of fusing.

The Properties of Glass During Firing

Glass, when exposed to high temperatures, will always move, expand, and contract. During the firing cycle, glass becomes soft, then viscous, and finally molten.

To fuse glass successfully, it is important to know what is taking place inside the kiln during the firing process. To help you to control the glass during firing, it is necessary to understand the stages of glass movement by observing visual changes in the kiln. The best source of information will be gained by opening the kiln and taking accurate notes of your observations during firing sessions.

The adjacent information chart describes the various stages of both Bullseye clear glass and sheet window glass as they heat and mature to the full-fuse state. The temperatures noted will be accurate if your pyrometer is adjusted properly (see "Pyrometer," Chapter 4). The most precise monitoring of glass during fusing is often direct and visual. The successful fusing of glass is dependent upon careful observation of the glass while it is being fired.

Mixing Colors

There are many ways to achieve different colors when fusing together two or more glasses. The following concepts become very apparent after gaining a little hands-on experience.

1) Generally speaking, the color-wheel concept of mixing colors is applicable when overlaying different colored glasses. Minor changes will become readily apparent. Bullseye #SP311 transparent pink will act very much like red when mixed with other colors. Red cathedral #122 is so intense that when fused, the red further intensifies and darkens, overpowering other colors.

2) By overlaying clear Bullseye #101F on any color, that color will become less dense because the clear #l0lF sinks into the lower base color, thinning the base glass.

3) When placing yellow cathedral over blue cathedral, the overlapped section will be green. Of course, the intensity of the blue and yellow will determine the hue of the green that is produced. To take this method one step further, clear #101F may be placed on top of the yellow which is over the blue, creating two distinct shades of green (see Figure 109).

4) When using white opal (Bullseye #133) as the base of your piece (the bottom blank) and overlaying cathedral glasses, the fused surface will look glassy and deep. Light transmission will increase because the white opal base was thinned by the cathedral glass. By mixing different cathedrals and overlaying on white, the result will be like that of color-wheel mixing (i.e., when yellow and blue are over-lapped and placed on top of white, the area of overlap will be green).

Layering for Color Effect

The top glass displaces the base glass, making the cross section of the base glass thinner (Figure 107). The white base glass is displaced by the overlapping glass, forcing the base glass to fill in the voids (Figure 106).

CROSS SECTIONS OF GLASS

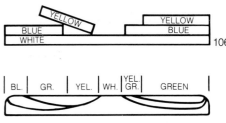

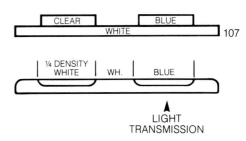

LIGHT TRANSMISSION

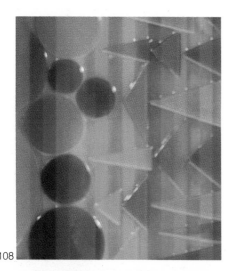

108

109

110

108. Frances and Michael Higgins. *Piece showing the subtle variations of color made possible by overlapping various transparent glasses.*

109. *Color layering over white opalescent glass. From the left: 1 layer of clear, 1 layer of blue, 1 layer of yellow partially laid over blue, yellow completely covering blue.*

The diamond-cut edge shows the displacement of the white opalescent bottom layer.

110. Cindy Macken. *Plaid bowl using yellow green as bottom layer; strips of transparent blue and red were placed on top. Note the different color hues attained from this simple combination.*

111. Diane Kinsey Busacker. *Platter, 3 layers of glasses: bottom of silver amber cathedral; second strips of iridized red and metal-flake green; top strips of clear, spaced 1/2" apart. The clear strips cause the red and green to move into the space between the clear layers, providing the textured appearance.*

111

Volume Control

The concept of volume control is best understood after observing the various shapes and thicknesses of glass as they go through the melting and fusing cycles. While progressing through the temperature range between 1450 and 1600 degrees F., glasses will gradually change in shape and volume. As the temperature increases, the volume equalizes across the entire shape of the piece. By understanding the gradual flow of glass, very accurate size control may be achieved.

One layer of glass with a design (e.g., a flower) laid over the top will fully fuse at approximately l500 degrees F. but will still have surface texture of varying thicknesses. If the glass is heated above l500 degrees F., it will start to pull up around the edges of the flower, and the outer shape of the original project will be altered.

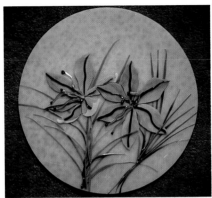

112

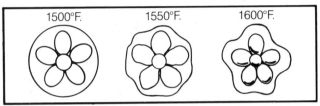 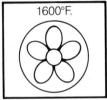

1 LAYER THICK + DESIGN   2 LAYERS THICK + DESIGN

113

However, if two layers of glass (blanks) are overlaid with the same flower design and fired to l600 degrees F., there will be no change in the outer shape because the volume of glass is at equilibrium with the surface tension. When the volume of any piece is approximately 2-1/4 layers, it can be fused flat, and the original two-dimensional size will not change...only the cross-section thickness will be re-arranged. Example: If an 8″ x 8″ tile is desired, stack two pieces cut to 8″ x 8″ and a third piece cut to 2″ x 2″...the resulting fused tile will measure 8″ x 8″.

The following techniques will become more apparent with experience when desiring to maintain a predetermined shape and size.

1) When designing a circular piece larger than 8 inches in diameter, cut the bottom blank 1/2 inch larger in diameter.

2) When placing a cut-piece design on two layers, keep the design at least 3/4″ from the edge (see Figure 112, Mike Barton floral).

3) Slow the firing at l500 degrees F. (instead of firing to l600 degrees F.) and soak for 15-20 minutes; a more even glass flow will result.

4) When 1/4-inch holes are drilled in both layers of glass and aligned, they will round off but will not flow together.

114

112. The greatest weight of the design is placed at least ¾″ from the edge to prevent the volume from distorting the shape of the outside edge.

113. Volume test before firing, showing the layers of the different glasses.

114. After fusing to flat.

116. Each of these crosses started out the same size; the top row has one layer of glass, and the bottom row has two layers. From left to right, three different shapes of glass were created by different fusing temperatures: the pieces in the left column were fired to 1450°F.; the pieces in the center column were fired to 1500°F.; pieces in the right column were fired to 1600°F.

115

115. These cut circles started out being equal in diameter: the yellow one was fired to 1450°F., the red one to 1500°F., and the black to 1600°F.

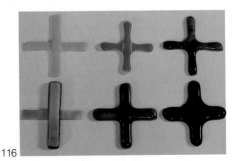

116

Techniques of Firing

Firing Fast

Initiate with a fast rise in temperature to full fuse (1600 to 1625 degrees F.) followed by a rapid drop to anneal. Total time should be one hour. Hold and soak, then turn off kiln and allow it to cool at its own rate.

Firing with Moderation

Begin with a moderate rise to fuse and hold kiln at 1500 degrees F. for 15 minutes, watching maturation of surface. Moderate temperature fall to anneal soak for 45 minutes, dropping through the anneal zone slowly but constantly. Turn off kiln and allow it to cool at its own rate.

Firing with Kiln Comprehension

Understand the firing characteristics of your kiln under specific conditions and learn how to utilize them properly. Example: When a set of plates was fired in the Bullseye/Octagon, an 11" blank with cut design was placed on a kiln shelf 1 inch from the floor. Using a 012 cone in the kiln sitter, the kiln was set on "high," and the lid was vented 1/2 inch. After 1 hour the kiln was closed, and approximately 1 hour later turned off by the kiln sitter. The kiln was again vented for 1/2 hour using 1" kiln posts, then closed. Six inches of home fiber glass insulation was then placed on the top of the lid. (The insulation was added when the kiln was still above the annealing temperature, but below the devitrification range. This was done in order to slow the cooling enough to anneal glass over 1/4" in thickness.) This method became a routine, and was so time-efficient that other firings or designing could take place without worry.

Test your own preferred method by stacking three 2" squares; check for stress after firing. If the three layers of clear glass anneal, you are assured your piece and all similar pieces will anneal.

Firing with Money

Determine the desired firing cycle and use an automatic controller to fire the kiln from start to finish.

Conclusion

Once the artist understands the properties of glass and has the opportunity to observe the nature of glass during the fusing process, he can begin to create individual character in his own work. Advanced processes are dependent upon utilizing and controlling basic techniques. Fusing begins by using cold glass; the fuser brings life to the glass by providing heat and individual expression.

ANNEALING

CHAPTER 7

Annealing and the Idealized Fusing Cycle

The continued success of fusing glass projects is directly related to a clear understanding of the heating (fusing) and cooling (annealing) characteristics of glass. This chapter is designed to give the reader a theoretical understanding of these fundamentals. To accomplish this, a simplified firing schedule (graph), called the Idealized Fusing Cycle, is set up and discussed (illustrated on pages 52 and 53).

There are six stages in the idealized fusing cycle: two for heating (initial heat and rapid heat), and four for cooling (rapid cool, anneal soak, anneal cool, and cool to room temperature). At first glance, this graph of the various stages may appear quite complex...even frightening! Don't let this scare you away. It will all become quite simple in time. Annealing, which occurs in the latter part of the cycle, is most important to understand if the fuser wants to advance beyond creating only very simple, small, or thin pieces.

Simply stated, annealing is the controlled cooling of glass to eliminate and prevent unwanted stress in the finished piece. Unwanted stress is the culprit that will eventually cause the glass to crack. It is impossible to remove all stress from glass; in fact, it is desirable to have some compressive stress existing on the outer surfaces of the piece with corresponding tensile stress in the inner layers. This situation contributes to a stronger and more durable piece of glass. (See diagram on page 55.) Fortunately, this situation tends to occur naturally due to the manner in which glass cools.

The final stress situation in glass is determined by (and only by) the cooling process through the annealing range. Understanding annealing becomes more critical to success when fusing thick or very large pieces; also, glasses with higher expansion coefficients require more careful annealing than those with lower expansion coefficients. The principles of annealing presented here can be applied to all forms of hot worked glass including cast and blown glass.

Annealing is best achieved in the simplest manner (i.e., to take advantage of the natural cooling cycle which occurs as the kiln cools). Complex cooling cycles are neither necessary nor recommended unless unsuccessful results occur when using simple cycles. For most pieces of reasonable size and less than 3/16″ thick, simple cycles work well. The theory discussed in this chapter is introduced to enable the fuser to better solve cracking problems as they occur by making more intelligent adjustments to a firing schedule. By referring to the idealized cycle, one can deduce where and how to change the cooling cycle. We recommend approaching annealing by firing a clear test glass specimen of the desired thickness through a particular cycle and viewing the amount of stress with a Stressometer. If excessive stress exists, the cycle can be altered until the desired results are achieved. The amount of excess stress that is tolerable in a piece of glass depends upon its use. If, after fusing, it is to be cut with a diamond saw or ground and polished, the less stress the better. At the Fusing Ranch we like to test for adequate annealing by subjecting the fused piece to repeated cycles in a dishwasher. (This is not recommended for those glasses with an expansion coefficient higher than that of Bullseye glass.)

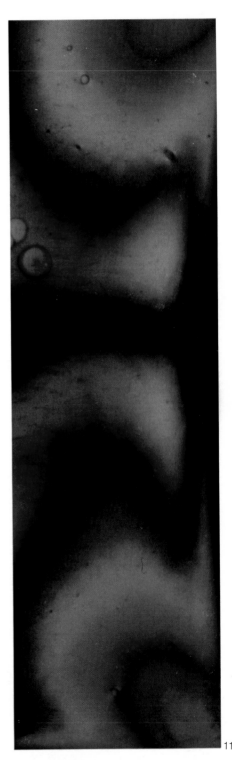

117

117. Stress patterns in a 1″-thick slab of glass viewed through a large Stressometer. Actual dimensions are 16″ x 9¼″ x 1″.

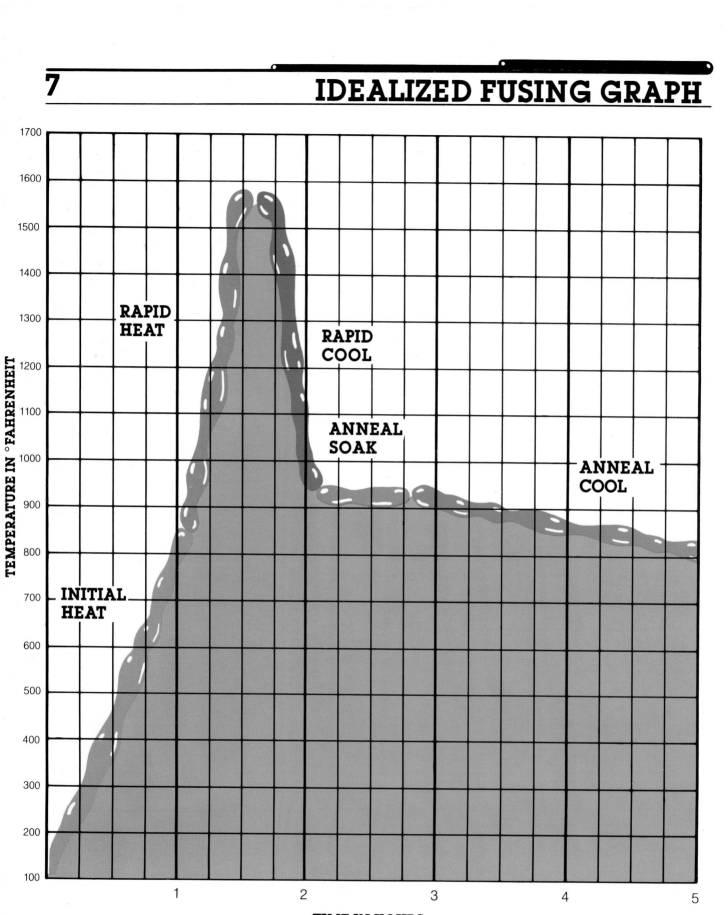

FUSED (in.) THICKNESS	ANNEAL TEMP. (°F)	ANNEALING TIME	TRANSITION RATE (°F/min)
1/8"	930	30 min	50
3/16"	915	30 min	25
1/4"	900	30 min	13
5/16"	890	45 min	8.8
3/8"	880	45 min	6.0
7/16"	870	60 min	4.5
1/2"	860	90 min	3.4

FUSED THICKNESS   vs.   ANNEALING DATA

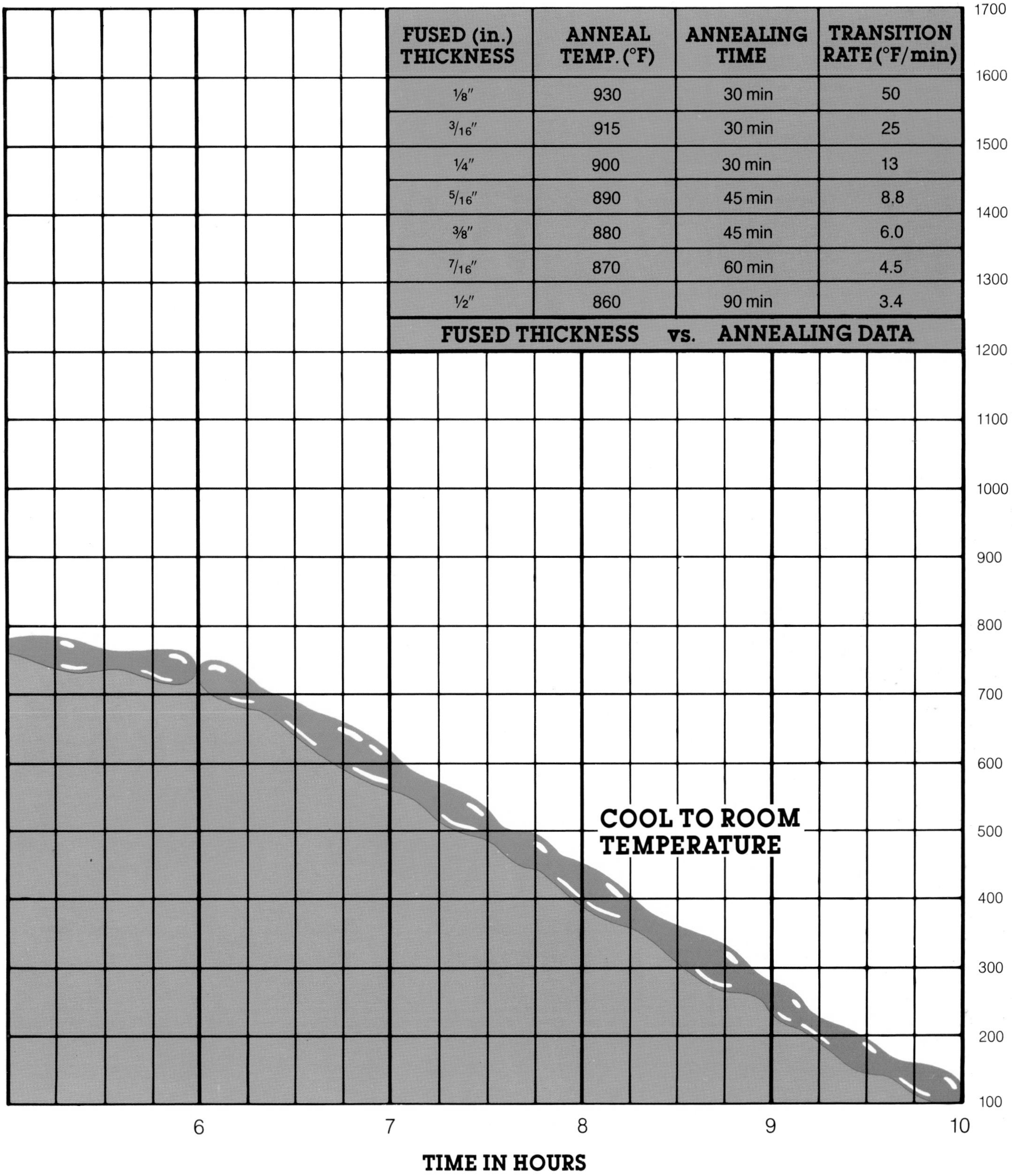

COOL TO ROOM TEMPERATURE

TIME IN HOURS

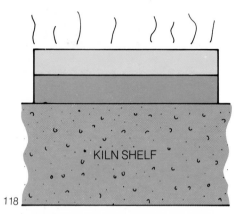

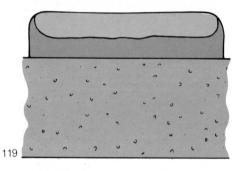

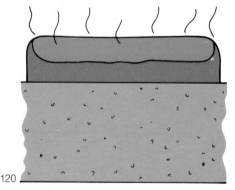

118. *Initial heat. Initiate with a slow rise to the strain point temperature of the glass. The glass is expelling moisture, and organic material such as glue is burning off. The kiln should be vented slightly during this stage.*

119. *Rapid heat to climax. Continue to heat from the strain point temperature to desired fusing level. To prevent devitrification, the temperature rise should be accomplished as quickly as possible.*

120. *Rapid cool should also be accomplished quickly until the annealing range temperature has been reached. Open the kiln door to vent off heat quickly.*

Initial Heat

Initial heat is the stage which consists of heating the unfused layers of glass from room temperature to just above the strain point temperature. In colored glasses, this temperature may range from 750 to 900 degrees F. Above the strain point, glass physically acts like a liquid and will not crack due to extreme heating rates. Generally, glass can be heated during this initial heat stage at a rate just below the temperature rate that would cause shattering. This rate varies with the dimension of the thickest single layer of glass. For 1/8″ layers this is quite rapid—as fast as 200 degrees F./minute. However, other variables such as expelling moisture, preventing excessive bubbles, maturing an overglaze or enamel, type of kiln, etc. need to be taken into consideration, perhaps requiring much slower heating rates. As there is little to gain and much to lose by a rapid initial heat, a temperature rise of 15 to 25 degrees F./minute is a workable rate of increase. Once the strain point is reached, stage 2 begins.

Rapid Heat

Rapid heat is the process of heating the unfused glass layers from the strain point temperature to the temperature at which the individual glass layers have fused to the desired level. This stage of the heating cycle, in contrast to the initial heat stage, should be accomplished more rapidly.

Opalescent glasses and some cathedrals have a tendency to devitrify (causing a crystalline scum on the surface) during the firing process. This can usually be avoided by spending as little time as possible at temperatures above 1300 degrees F.; therefore, the kiln should be designed with sufficient heating power to allow rapid heating from 1000 to 1600 degrees F. It is important to note that progressing slowly in some circumstances is beneficial (as in the anneal cooling stage), while in others it can be quite detrimental. It could be detrimental to slowly raise the kiln temperature from 1000 to 1600 degrees F. over a four-hour period because the likelihood of devitrification would be very high for most glasses. Once the desired fuse is achieved, the next stage begins.

Rapid Cool

Cooling the fused glass from the highest temperature reached during the rapid heat stage to the optimum annealing temperature is referred to here as rapid cool. There is nothing to gain by going slowly through this zone. To insure against devitrification, this cooling stage should be carried out as rapidly as the kiln will allow. This is usually achieved by opening the kiln door for 5 to 10 minutes to quickly vent off heat. If you are working with glasses that do not easily devitrify, rapid cool is of less concern, and slower cooling is acceptable...the limit being the rate where devitrification occurs. Once the rapid cool temperature stage reaches the annealing range (approximately 1000 degrees F.), stage 4 begins.

Annealing Soak Time

Temperature zone 4, or annealing soak, is the process of holding the kiln at a constant temperature (the optimum annealing temperature) for a given time for a given thickness of glass. Soak times and temperatures for various fused glass thicknesses (from 1/8″ to 1/2″) are shown on the Table on page 53. For the purpose of control and convenience, Bullseye glasses were used in the formulation of this Table; however, other glasses of a compatible molecular structure may render similar results. During the annealing soak, two important things happen: the temperature of the mass of glass and the temperature of the kiln shelf are allowed to equalize, and any stress in the glass due to uneven heating or mechanical working (e.g., sagging or combing) is relieved. Once the recommended annealing soak time has passed, stage 5 begins.

Anneal Cool

This zone is bounded by the annealing soak temperature (on the top end) and the strain point (on the lower end). It is during this stage (and only this stage) when the development of permanent stress in the final piece of glass can be prevented. Glass in this zone is slowly becoming more rigid, but is not yet stiff enough to act like a solid. The cooling rate through this transition will directly affect the amount of permanent stress in the final piece. (See Table on page 53 for anneal cooling rates.)

Being conservative helps here...the more slowly you progress through this zone, the less stress will appear in the final piece. Once the glass is below the strain point temperature, the remaining cooling rate does not affect the stress condition in the final piece.

Cool to Room Temperature

The process of cooling to room temperature need only proceed slowly enough to prevent shattering. The maximum allowable cooling rate to prevent shattering is dependent upon thickness, but it is generally quite fast. Therefore, the natural cooling rate of the kiln is usually more than adequate for pieces less than 1/2″ thick. Cooling at slower rates has no effect on the final stress. Generally, kilns are allowed to cool naturally overnight, with the peephole or the door partially opened to promote quicker cooling.

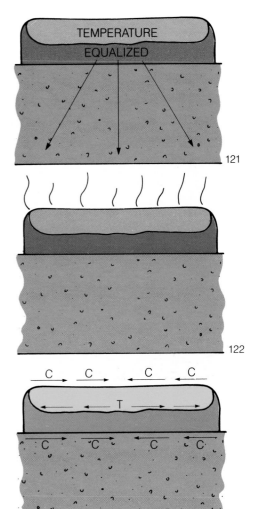

121

122

123

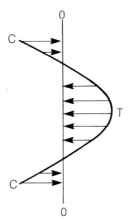

STRESS CROSS SECTION

121. Anneal soak. Hold the kiln at this constant temperature to allow both the glass and the kiln shelf temperatures to equalize.

122. Anneal cool. Slowly decrease the temperature to avoid developing any permanent stress. During this stage, the glass is contracting: the outer surface is shrinking more than the inside, which yields plastically.

123. Cool to room temperature. After the strain point, decrease the temperature slowly enough to prevent shattering. At this time the glass is becoming rigid, the inside layer is under tension putting the outer layers in compression, creating a balance that will prevent cracking or shattering in the end product.

Testing Glass for Determination of the Annealing Range

If the annealing range of a glass is not readily available from the manufacturer, use the slump method to determine the proper temperature range: 1) Cut a strip of glass 3/8″ wide by 12″ long. 2) Place the glass strip over two bricks spaced 10 inches apart in the annealing oven. More than one glass may be tested at one time. (See Figure 124.) 3) Bring the kiln temperature up slowly, watching the pyrometer constantly once it is above 900 degrees F. For the most accurate test, the kiln temperature should rise at 9 degrees per minute after reaching 900 degrees F. 4) When the glass has sagged 1/2 inch, read the pyrometer and subtract 60 degrees F.; this is the upper limit of the annealing range. The lower limit of the range (just above the strain point) is 150 degrees F. below the upper limit. This 150-degree range is referred to as the annealing range. The optimum annealing temperature usually lies midway in this range but should be determind by trial. For Bullseye and many other commercial colored sheet glasses, the annealing range is 150 degrees F.; however, glasses with ranges as narrow as 100 degrees F. and as wide as 200 degrees F. exist. Whenever possible, obtain annealing information directly from the manufacturer.

124. Slump test of nine different Bullseye glasses shown in the Marathon kiln. Note that some glasses are touching the shelf and others have just started to slump. In this test, there was a 60-degree F. temperature differential between the first glass and the last glass to slump. This would indicate a need to lengthen the annealing range if the first and last glasses to slump in this test were to be fused in the same piece.

124

DESIGN CHAPTER 8

Thus far, we have seen many beautiful examples of both loose and tight design that various glass artists have achieved through a variety of techniques. The variables that one needs to understand to create exciting designs can be few or many. Obviously the more variables and techniques mastered in glass fusing, the more opportunity for creative expression. We have witnessed an explosion of creativity in glass fusing during the past two years, both by stained glass artists breaking free of lead boundaries, and by craftspeople new to glass fusing. Whatever your current level of interest or experience in glass, many exciting design challenges await you.

In this chapter we will show, primarily through examples, some basic techniques and tips for designing a piece of fused glass. Photos showing techniques such as positive and negative design, repetitive patterns, and phase shift will be illustrated.

125. Finished jewelry made by Diane Kinsey Busacker.

126. Klaus Moje, *striped bowl using a simple design technique. See page 64.*

127. Classroom projects showing a variety of designs achieved by using simple fusing techniques.

125

126

127

128

129

130

128. Pink plate and two bowls using phase-shift design.

129. Cut blank and consecutive strips from one sheet of streaky glass, ready for assembly. When these strips are arranged in order, but with a slight phase shift, a design technique is accomplished.

130. Phase-shift pattern, laid out and ready for trimming into round shapes before fusing flat.

131. Phase-shift designs which have been fused flat, ready for slumping. Note the character of the individual strips and the phase-shift design created with this simple technique.

132. Same as Figure 131, set up next to slumping molds.

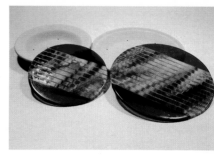

131

132

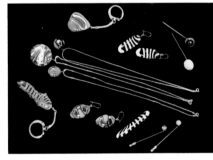

133. Jewelry by Tommy Ann Wolcott: Fusing fashion. Note outline of the cadmium/selenium red next to the aqua blue.

134. Figure 135 before fusing. Note that the black and white striped pieces are cut from pre-fused objects.

135. Jewelry set on shelf after firing. This shelf contains small pieces molded into fiber; cross sections of pre-fused pieces and sections of Bullrods.

136. Finished jewelry: stick pins, necklaces, and key chains.

137

138

137. Laying up a modular design on a white blank. The 15" circular blank has already been placed on the kiln shelf. After free-hand scoring, the backside of the second blank of dark red glass was placed between two sections of newspaper (scored side down). By applying pressure to the top of the blank through the newspaper, the circular blank broke into varied squares. Using this method, a modular design becomes easy to transfer to the base blank.

138. Using some of the small squares created from the second blank, a design was created using the white glass as negative space. On top of the dark red squares, a few orange squares and an occasional clear square were placed to add depth and to create enough volume so the piece would remain circular after fusing.

139. Spray "A" overglaze was applied to the surface to insure against devitrification.

140. Close-up of modular design showing random thickness and an even coating of Spray "A."

141. Finished piece after full fuse to flat. This piece was fired to 1550 degrees F. and held for 15 minutes.

139

140

141

142

143

144

145

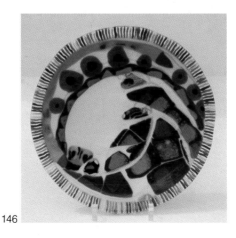

146

142. Cut-out of Figure 141 with sanded edges, ready for slumping.

143. Finished modular-design bowl. The fused piece was cut into a smaller circle before slumping.

144. Constructing a plate from leftover scrap and cut-offs from previously fused pieces. Note the diversity of thickness and size of the piece prior to fusing; yet when fused to flat, volume will equalize across the entire piece.

145. Applying Spray "A" overglaze to free-form design plate.

146. Don't refuse "re-fusing!" This finished, fully-fused blank is the culmination of scraps from previous pieces. Note that some of the design comes from the piece cut from the project shown in Figure 141.

147.

147. *Worktable layout of two design ideas which came from leaf patterns.*

148. *After cutting leaves out of Bullseye #112 green, they were laid out on a 16" blank of Bullseye #123 orange. The leaves were traced on fiber paper, as shown on the dark red blank which will be used as the bottom blank.*

149. *Leaf project glued up and ready for placement on the kiln shelf. A dark red blank is the first layer; #123 orange and white comprise the second layer; #112 green leaves and the fiber paper were then glued to the surface of the #112 green. The leaf veins were cut with an Exacto knife. The project was placed with fiber next to the kiln shelf (i.e., topside down). In this way, the weight of the blank forces the glass to flow around and in between the fiber, adding texture to the finished piece.*

150. *Figure 149 after fusing, showing the results of overfiring. Although this was not the intended texture, the piece, as is, has its own unique beauty.*

151. *Close-up of plate showing depth of relief created by fiber impression.*

152. *The leaf design was accomplished with two 15" blanks. One dark green blank was cut into both a positive and a negative design. Half of the positive-design pieces were arranged and glued to one side of a tan blank (which appears gray in the photo).*

153. *Close-up of the finished palm leaf design showing texture created by fiber impression.*

154. *Palm leaf design, laid up, showing positive design pattern with stem in place. Fiber paper has been glued to the dark green leaf shapes and will be fired with the design side down.*

148

149

151

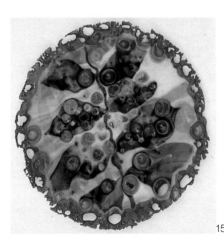

150

155. *Note the simplicity of achieving a design on both sides of the plate by using just two pieces of glass. This piece, glued up and ready for placement on the kiln shelf, shows the negative design from the dark green leaves.*

156. *Finished Palm Leaf plate.*

152

153

154

155

156

157

158

159

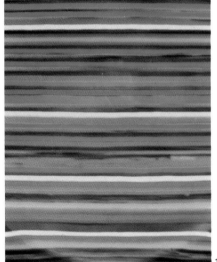

160

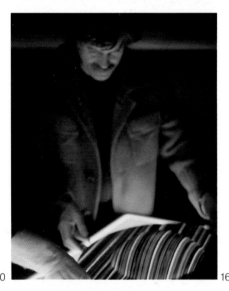

161

157. Klaus Moje working with ⅜" cut strips. Strips ⅜"x 19" are laid on edge and arranged on the prepared kiln shelf. A small piece of fiber contains the two outside edges, holding the strips upright.

158. Klaus Moje carrying the finished laid-up piece across the studio to the kiln. When many pieces have been arranged with no glue to hold them in place, transporting to the kiln can be challenging.

159. Klaus Moje loading strip design into Bullseye/Marathon kiln.

160. Close-up of striped bowl after slumping, showing integrity of line achieved by holding the kiln at 1525 degrees F. for a 20-minute soak. This procedure keeps the lines of the glasses from moving or flowing into each other.

161. Klaus Moje views the slumped piece on a large polarimeter, checking for stress in the clear areas.

162. Finished strip-design bowl form by Klaus Moje.

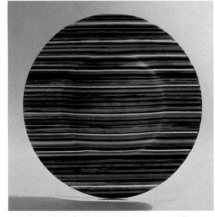

162

163

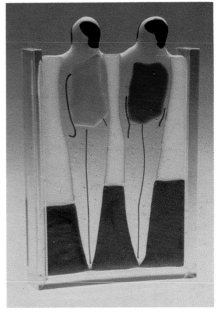

166

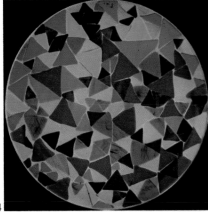

164

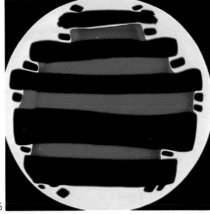

165

163. Ronnie Wolf, "Searching," 9" x 9", 1982. The display of this fused tile was considered part of the original design concept. The frame contains a fragment of a street scene. It becomes apparent that there is more outside the frame; therefore, the frame becomes less dominant.

164. David Ruth, 16" platter, 1982. The use of repetitive triangles and a limited color palette maintain simplicity in the concept; yet, it is dynamic in scope. This could be the first platter in a series by changing one color at a time; or by changing the size of the triangles, new designs would slowly evolve.

165. David Ruth, 16" platter, 1982. Laying out rectangles on a circle with contrasting small pieces is a similar concept to the multiple-triangle platter. Here, the rectangles are the dominant design element, but the positive variations in design are as great as with the triangles. The use of negative space is not as dominant in this piece.

166. Ronnie Wolf, "Where's the Bus," 10" x 7", 1982. Similar to Figure 163. If any limits exist with this design and display technique, it is that the pieces are one-sided.

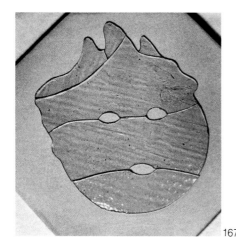

167

168

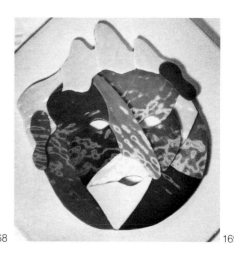

169

170

This series (Figures 167 through 172) shows the steps used by Ruth Brockmann in the construction of a mask.

167. Clear glass base, cut and assembled, leaving voids for the mouth and eyes. It is not necessary for the base to be clear; it could be any other compatible color.

168. Layout of second color overlays shows the pieces before they are overlapped.

169. If you look closely at this photograph, you can see how the various pieces are stacked. Some are arranged like shingles (the hair). The nose is the last piece, stacked on top, creating dimension.

170. Ruth Brockmann adds the final small line detail using tweezers and glue. Fused masks in the background have not been slumped.

171. Full-fused mask before slumping. Note how eyes and mouth have rounded off.

172. Finished mask after slumping over a curved face mold.

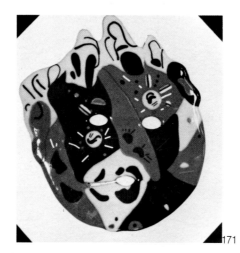

171

172

QUALITIES OF VARIOUS GLASSES   CHAPTER 9

"To preserve, within a given form, the robust nobility of the hot, thick glass ready to be blown, and while blowing it, to let the nature of the glass assert itself, to control its natural tendencies without denying them; while the glass is at the height of its incandescence, to coax from it forms that are plump and yielding, and then to incorporate into them other feelings evoking still or running water, or cracking and melting ice."

This quote, from the autobiography of Maurice Marinot, a French glassblower of the Art Nouveau era, describes the qualities of hot glass. Although fusing begins by using cold glass and breathing life into it with heat, the cold glass was born with the same hot, robust nobility of which Marinot speaks. The hot-forming process in the manufacturing of the different sheet glasses "freezes in" specific characteristics unique to each method. Following is a brief presentation of various glasses which are available to the fuser, their intrinsic characteristics, and their relationship to fusing.

Colored Glasses

Colored glasses are available in opalescent (translucent) and cathedral (transparent) colors as well as combinations of the two. These glasses can be further classified into types according to the production process used by the manufacturer: blown, drawn, and rolled.

Blown glasses include the various antique glasses such as Fisher, Lambert, St. Gobain, DeSag, and Fremont. These glasses are made by flattening cylinders that were blown from hand-gathered glass on a blowpipe. The hand-forming process gives these glasses unique qualities. This method allows the "flashing" of a thin color layer over a transparent or opal glass. Surface tool marks on a glassy surface, elongated bubbles, and occasional blisters characterize this glass.

Drawn glasses are referred to as "machine antique" and resemble blown glass, with the exception that the drawn process does not readily lend itself to making flashed colors. In general, these glasses do not have the subtle variations or wonderful blisters of the full antiques, but they are considerably less expensive than their blown counterparts.

Rolled glasses are produced primarily in the U.S.A. and are usually formed between two rollers, or like Bullseye glass, formed on a cast-iron table using only one roller. In general, the rolled glasses are most suitable for fusing because they are less expensive. The sought-after qualities of the more expensive antiques—mainly the free blown surfaces, the fine tool marks (stria), and the recognizable bubbles—are lost in the fusing process.

The full antiques, however, allow subtle sandblasting techniques to be incorporated into the fused design. The subtle color and tone changes provide the artist with a pre-made wash that is as subtle as watercolor. It would be very difficult to achieve this using anything but flashed glasses.

Since most intrinsic characteristics of the glass are lost during the fusing process, color and compatibility should be the key factors when selecting glasses for fusing.

173. These colors represent the glasses by number which are listed on the Bullseye glass sheet. Due to the light transmission quality of glass, many of the glasses have subtle color shifts depending on the light source.

Cathedral

101 clear
102 streak-clear/red
103 cherry red
104 streak-yellow/red
1105 light plum
1107 light green
1108 marine blue
1109 root beer brown
1112 deep forest green
1120 cadmium yellow
122 selenium red-orange
128 purple/light blue opal streak
129 gray/white opal streak
130 clear/white opal streak
1128 deep royal purple
1129 gray

Opalescent

100 black
105 blue opal/plum streak
106 white opal/caramel streak
107 white opal/light green streak
108 light blue/marine blue streak
109 white opal/root beer brown streak
110 caramel
110D chocolate brown
112 light green/opal/deep green streak
113 white opal
114 cobalt blue opal
115 caramel/deep forest green streak
116 turquoise blue
117 chrome green
118 white opal/cobalt blue opal streak
119 white opal/light plum streak
120 cadmium yellow opal
121 cadmium yellow opal/green streak
123 white opal/selenium orange streak
124 poppy red
125 selenium orange peel
126 lime green opal
127 leaf green opal/cherry red streak
131 white opal/cherry red streak
132 cream white
133 bone white

Specialty

SP111 soft silver yellow opal
SP200 streak peacock
SP250 streak peacock light
SP301 Gold pink opal
SP302 Gold pink opal through white opal
SP310 Gold pink cathedral through white
SP311 Gold pink cathedral

IR 122

IR 1112

1104

1120

1107

RP 108

IR RP 122

1112

1116

1108

IR RP 100

STR 1128

1114

1128

1105

SP 111

SP 200

103

122

1109

SP 250

C403

1129

101

102

130

129

128

104

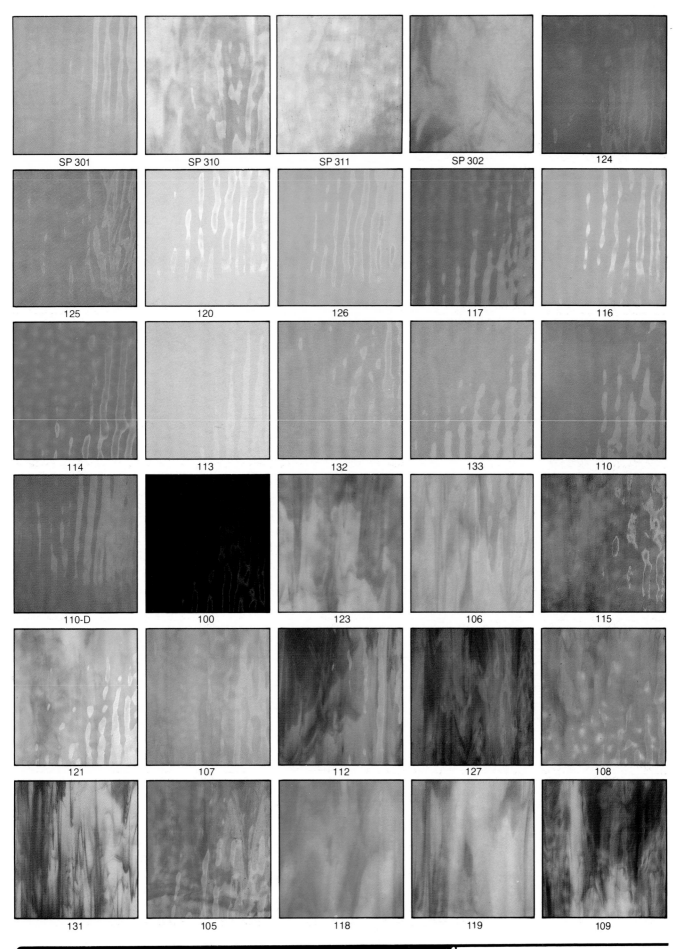

SP 301   SP 310   SP 311   SP 302   124

125   120   126   117   116

114   113   132   133   110

110-D   100   123   106   115

121   107   112   127   108

131   105   118   119   109

Commercial Window Glass

Clear window glass is available in various thicknesses. In the USA today, it is all produced by the "float" process. This process consists of flowing the molten glass onto the surface of a bath of molten tin where it spreads to a sheet of uniform thickness producing an excellent fire-polished surface. It is all "plate" quality and readily available in thickness of 3/32" (known as single strength), 1/8" (known as double strength), 3/16", 1/4", 5/16", 3/8", and 1/2". Generally, float glass is not compatible with any of the colored glasses currently being manufactured. (See "Expansion Coefficient Chart", page 44.)

Bottle Glass

Bottle glass is available in a myriad of shapes everywhere from the farthest reaches of the Grand Tetons to the nearest trash bin. The color palette is basically limited to clear, brown, green, and blue; yet, the use of this palette can be both challenging and rewarding. Expansion coefficients of bottle glass have been measured at the Fusing Ranch and range from 85 to 91; thus, bottle glass will fit the full range of expansion coefficients from float plate to Bullseye glass. Since glass is just a raw material to the fuser, bottle glass should not be disregarded.

Other Specialty Glasses

Iridescent glasses display lustrous, rainbow-like colors on the glass surfaces in the presence of reflected light. This phenomenon is the result of constructive/destructive light interference caused by a very thin film on the surface of the glass. There are two types of iridescent glasses available: carnival and metallic matte. *Carnival iridescent glasses* have a very shiny surface (similar to the appearance of a thin oil film on water) and are reminiscent of carnival blown glass. Iridescent glass of this type (Merry Go Round and Armstrong) are produced by spraying an organic compound such as tetra-isopropyl titanate on the surface of the glass after the sheet has been formed and is cooling (from 1000 to 800 degrees F.). Some of these glasses maintain their iridescence when sagged, but this surface will always burn off when fused. *Metallic matte iridescent glasses* (Bullseye) exhibit a rich, micro-crystalline surface similar to that of Tiffany and Frederick Carder blown art glass. This surface is produced by spraying a metallic chloride solution on the surface of the glass at the time the sheet is formed (1500 degrees F.) The sheet is then re-heated and stretched to break up the metallic crystalline surface. Metallic iridescence does not burn off during the sagging or fusing process.

Mottled glasses such as the catspaw of Bullseye glass and the large mottles of Uroboros and Oceana glasses are created by differential cooling of a specific glass formulation. Unfortunately, these mottles, which are so wonderful in the cold sheet, disappear when sagged or fused.

Conclusion

The various glasses discussed above by no means comprise a complete or comprehensive list of glasses and their qualities. It is hoped the reader will realize that many of the characteristics of these various glasses are lost or changed in the fusing process. Therefore, the fuser should be more interested in the properties of these glasses after the fusing process has been performed.

KILNS

CHAPTER 10

Heat is the catalyst that makes glass fusing possible. The kiln provides the heat which, when properly controlled, will cause glass to move through its various stages from room temperature to molten and back again. A kiln must have the capacity to heat glass to at least 1600 degrees F. and to provide a means of monitoring, controlling, and observing the various stages of firing. Types of kilns and devices for firing and monitoring kilns are described in this chapter; however, only electric kilns are discussed. Gas kilns can be used for fusing but are more involved to install and operate. A permit is usually required to plumb the gas piping and to install the exhaust flue. In contrast, the electric kilns discussed herein are ready to use by simply plugging them into standard house appliance receptacles. A small or medium-sized electric kiln provides the best value and convenience for the majority of users for whom this book was intended.

Kilns Available

The Fusing Ranch, in conjunction with two major kiln manufacturers, provides three kiln models specifically designed for fusing (see page 72). A typical side-fired kiln is the "Bullseye/Octagon 16," a 220-volt/15-amp model. This is an excellent kiln for studios seeking versatility. It includes a kiln sitter which acts as an automatic shut-off for production or classroom firing. The nine-inch depth allows two octagonal kiln shelves to be fired at one time, providing 400 square inches of usable shelf space. For greater slumping versatility, a single shelf allows a nine-inch slumping depth. This kiln is top-loading (with a removable lid), comes with a metal stand, a pyrometer, two kiln shelves, and an infinite switch for controlling the rate of temperature climb. To ensure easy installation, a female receptacle or power cord adapter is included. (There are over 15 manufacturers of this type of kiln.) Most ceramic bisque kilns have a similar construction and are available through ceramic supply shops.

The Fusing Ranch offers two top-fired kilns: the "Bullseye/Marathon" and the "Pinto." The Bullseye/Marathon has the advantages of a large shelf size (400 square inches) and a rapid heating rate. The Marathon is rated at 220 volts/30 amps, so special wiring may be necessary for home use; however, most houses are wired for 220 volts (clothes dryers and electric stoves use 220-volt current). With the Marathon, enamel temperatures can be reached in 20 minutes, and full-fuse temperatures reached in 30 minutes if desired. It is constructed with ceramic fiber insulation in a sturdy, solid metal chassis, and includes a table top stand. The Marathon is front-loading, has two infinite switches, and an effective slumping depth of five inches.

The Pinto is top-loading, top-fired, and has a slumping depth of six inches. Its main advantage is its simplicity. The Pinto operates on only 14 amps of 110-volt current and can be plugged into any outlet in your house. It comes with a pyrometer, an infinite switch, a 13-1/2" diameter kiln shelf, and a welded stand.

Denver Glass Machinery markets two top-loading, top-fired kilns: the KL-50 (42 x 30 inches) and the KL-27 (21 x 21 inches), which are rated at 220 volts/30 amps.

Glass Fusion Studio sells plans and materials for a do-it-yourself kiln. When assembled, this kiln is 18 x 18 inches on the inside, operates on 220-volt current, and has an infinite control switch. It is designed with a combination of insulating firebrick and insulating fiber blanket. Constructing your own kiln may be rewarding if satisfaction is gained from fabricating equipment.

This is not a complete list of available kilns. It includes only those kilns with

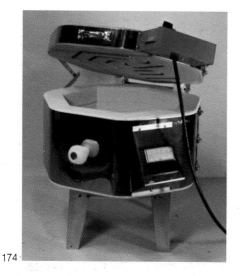

174

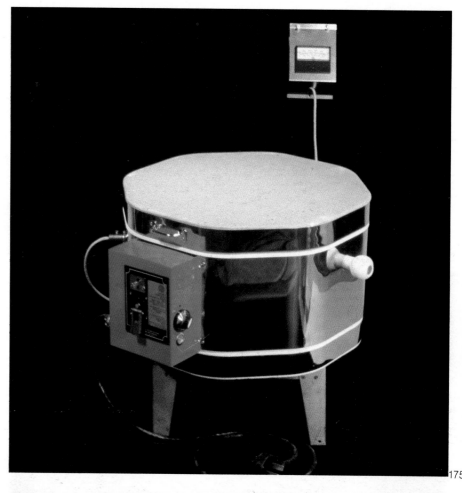

175

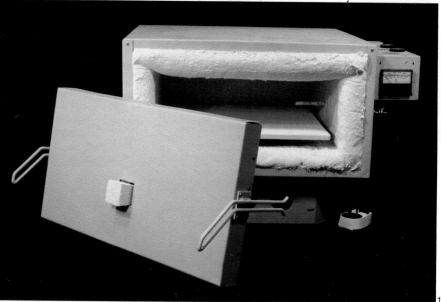

176

174. *Pinto (13 1/2"; 110 volt, 14 amps). This inexpensive kiln comes complete and ready to use. It may be plugged into any common household receptacle.*

175. *Bullseye/Octagon (16"; 220 volts/15 amps). This kiln is similar to most ceramic bisque kilns available through ceramic supply shops. It comes equipped with a kiln sitter, two shelves, a pyrometer, an infinite temperature control switch, and a stand.*

176. *Bullseye/Marathon (20" x 20"; 220 volts/30 amps). This is a top-fired, ceramic fiber-insulated kiln. It comes equipped with a shelf, a pyrometer, infinite temperature control switches, and a stand.*

179

180

177

181

178

which we have had experience or would otherwise recommend. The following description of types and constructions of kilns will give the reader insight into the selection of additional kilns suitable for fusing glass.

Kiln Types

Electric kilns may have heating elements located either on the inside top of the kiln (as in the Pinto and Bullseye/Marathon kilns) or around the inside walls of the kiln (as in the Bullseye/Octagon 16). (See Figure 183 on page 74 .) Kilns with heating elements on the top are called "top-fired." Kilns with heating elements around the sides are called "side-fired." The location and arrangement of the heating elements will determine how the glass is heated. A close look at how the glass receives the heat from the kiln elements will point out the important differences between fusing with a top-fired or a side-fired kiln.

177. Liz Mapelli's *studio kiln (20" x 40")*.

178. Denver Glass Machinery *kilns (left to right): KL-50 (42" x 30"), KL-27 (21" x 21")*.

179. *Homemade kiln (24" x 36") was built with surplus materials from Bullseye Glass Company by Rob Snyder.*

180. Ray Ahlgren's *studio kiln (20" x 40"). Note that the kiln floor is constructed on a roll-around table; the kiln chassis with the heating elements may be raised and lowered with a small hand winch attached to the studio ceiling.*

181. *Kiln chassis is raised to promote rapid cool.*

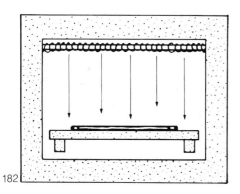

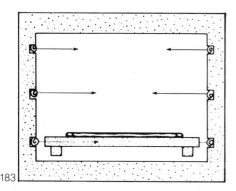

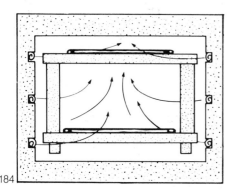

With a side-fired kiln, the heat radiates from the side walls (where the elements are located) to the center of the kiln. The kiln shelf also conducts heat in this same direction. Therefore, the glass on the outer perimeter of the shelf receives heat before the glass in the center of the shelf. This causes the temperature of the glass in the center to lag behind the temperature of the glass around the outer perimeter of the shelf during the initial heat-up. If this temperature difference is too great, unequal expansion of the glass will cause shattering. Because of this, the initial heat-up of the glass in the side-fired kiln must be much slower to prevent shattering.

Side-fired kilns do have the advantage of being capable of firing several shelves at one time. The spacing between shelves becomes very important if the same firing of all shelves is desired. Proper spacing between shelves will allow the same "heat soak" to be obtained on each shelf.

Top-fired kilns radiate heat downward from the elements over the entire surface of the glass on the shelf. All of the glass receives a similar quantity of heat at the same time. Therefore, since no temperature differences exist in the glass from the center to the outer perimeter, the expansion of the glass is uniform. This allows for a faster initial heat-up of the glass without cracking. (See diagrams on this page.)

Kiln Insulation

Kilns are usually insulated with one of two types of refractory insulation: insulating firebrick (known as "soft brick") and ceramic fiber insulation. (See definitions in 'Glassery.') Ceramic fiber is very lightweight and stores less heat during heat-up than does insulating firebrick. A kiln constructed of soft brick heats up more slowly than does the same kiln constructed of fiber. The soft brick absorbs more heat...a phenomenon known as "soaking." This property, which at first appears to be a disadvantage, can in many cases be used to your advantage. The soft brick will soak up more heat than the fiber in the heat-up cycle, but upon cooling will give some of this heat back to the kiln. This phenomenon is called "rebound." By selecting the proper thickness of soft brick when designing a kiln, the natural cooling will be slow enough so that the elements will not need to be fired at a low setting in order to achieve a slow cooling rate. In contrast, fiber-insulated kilns may require firing down during the annealing range in order to avoid losing heat too quickly.

Physical Construction

Basically, a kiln must be constructed with a door to enable objects to be placed in it with relative ease. There are two possible door locations for kilns: the door or lid on the top (called a top-loader), or the door in front (called a front-loader). A door can be as simple as a removable lid, or it may be hinged in any number of ways. Each has its pros and cons, but the simplest is usually the most functional. Top-loading kilns have the advantage of allowing easy access to the entire top surface of the fusing project. Front-loading ovens allow less access to the top, but provide a full view of the side which is advantageous in slumping and sagging. A front-loading, side-fired kiln with no elements on the door fires very unevenly and is not recommended for fusing.

Another physical requirement is the ability to view the glass through the stages of firing without substantial heat loss inside the kiln. This is accomplished by placing a peephole in the proper position.

The kiln must also have a means of venting off heat during cooling. Because

182. Illustration showing radiant heat transfer in a typical top-fired kiln.

183. Illustration showing radiant heat transfer in a typical side-fired kiln.

184. To obtain a uniform heat soak on both shelves, this illustration shows proper shelf placement when firing two shelves in a side-fired kiln.

heat rises, the venting of a top-loader is often more uniform than with front-loaders. A small wedge in the lid of the top-loader will allow excess heat to escape from around the entire circumference. Venting a front-loader may cause uneven heat loss, substantially cooling the fused item nearest the door. If a vent or large peephole is placed opposite the door, this problem can be partially alleviated (as was done in the case of the Bullseye/Marathon). Only when more than one peephole is present, on opposite sides of a kiln, can the peephole act as a vent.

The exterior chassis of a kiln may be constructed with a variety of materials. In the case of soft brick kilns, it is important that the bricks be held together by a compressive skin on the outside. This is necessary to keep the bricks from walking apart during the heating and cooling cycles. Most ceramic kilns on the market today use a modular design of nine-inch bricks arranged in a circular configuration. These kilns range in size from a 14-inch diameter to a 28-inch diameter; all are similar in construction to the Bullseye/Octagon.

Kiln Controls

The heat input of kilns must be controlled to obtain the proper heating and cooling rates. Electric kilns generally have one of two types of switches to control the flow of electricity to the elements. The first type is the "high/medium/low" switch. This switch is less desirable for fusing due to its limited control; however, these switches may be replaced with an infinite switch system quite easily. (See 'Glassery' for detailed information.) The second type, the infinite switch, has a knob with numbers ranging from 1 to 7 (number 1 being low, and number 7 being high). Each increasing number represents a larger percentage of time the elements will be on. Number 4, which is in the middle, indicates the power is on 50% of the time; number 7 indicates the elements are on 100% of the time. The percentage of "on" time is accomplished by cycling the power on for a number of seconds and then off for a number of seconds. An infinite switch indeed has infinite control. That is, a position halfway between "off" and number 1 equals 1/2; a position halfway between numbers 4 and 5 equals 4-1/2. This is not the case with the high/medium/low switches where any position between low, medium, or high is OFF. (Note: Due to the tolerances in the manufacturing of some infinite switches, the position "one-half low" may not provide any power to the elements. If this is the case, the same heat situation can be achieved by cracking the kiln door 1/8 inch and turning the switch to the "low" setting.) (See Chapter 11, "Firing the Kiln.")

The kiln sitter is a device used for shutting off power to the kiln at a predetermined top-end heat level. It may also serve as a safety device in case of overfiring. Complex as it may seem, the kiln sitter is designed to be simple and reliable. There are few moving parts, and you can adjust them for perfect operation yourself. A sensing rod rests on a small cone inside the kiln. When the cone softens, the weight of the rod bends it down, releasing a falling weight; the action of the falling weight turns off the kiln. If the small cone does not shut the kiln off at the proper time, simply adjust the trigger according to instructions. (See Figures 185, 186, and 187.)

One advantage of the kiln sitter as a shut-off device is the ability to achieve the same results whether firing rapidly or slowly, since the cone is designed to take the firing rate of the kiln into consideration. (See 'Glassery' for a detailed explanation of pyrometric cones.)

Other automatic controllers are commercially available. These devices can control the firing of a kiln in any firing cycle desired. The one drawback is that they

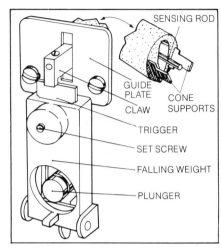

185

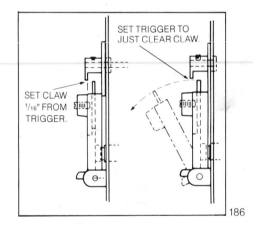

186

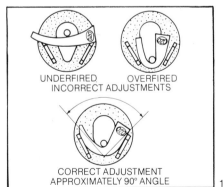

187

185. Perspective drawing of the various working parts of the kiln sitter and their appropriate part names.

186. Side views of the kiln sitter "claw" and "trigger" showing proper clearance.

187. End view of Junior cone configuration after firing, illustrating proper and improper adjustments.

188

189

are expensive. We call it "firing with money." Three types of automatic controllers are available: 1) a set-point controller which allows you to dial a control knob to the desired temperature (This controller automatically fires the elements to obtain the desired temperature.); 2) a cam controller which allows the complete firing schedule to be mapped out on a Plexiglas cam (This cam then instructs the controller to fire the kiln for the determined time and temperature cycle. Cam controllers are available in two models: one indicates the temperature on a dial, and the other actually graphs the temperature on a paper chart.); and 3) a programmable controller which allows you to control several ovens at one time with any number of possible firing schedules. This device uses a solid-state memory which can be programmed simply by punching in the desired time-temperature cycle on a small keyboard. Such a device is expensive but allows total versatility. (Examples of these types of automatic controllers are shown on this page.)

Pyrometers

Temperature is monitored with a device called the pyrometer. It is composed of a temperature-sensing device (the thermocouple) and a temperature indicator. The indicator is usually one of two types: galvanometric or potentiometric. (See 'Glassery' for an explanation of these two types of temperature indicators.)

Commercial kilns have the thermocouple properly located for accurate readings. The location of the thermocouple determines how closely the pyrometer reading represents the actual kiln temperature. (This is discussed in depth in Chapter 11.)

Conclusion

In this chapter, we have discussed various kilns available commercially as well as types of construction, insulation, and controls. It is hoped that this information will encourage the reader to acquire or build a kiln, since this is what is needed to become involved in fusing. To spend months looking for what you may think is the "best" kiln will not increase your knowledge or skill in fusing.

We recommend starting with an inexpensive kiln such as the Pinto. A pyrometer should be part of any kiln selected. Future kiln requirements will become obvious as your direction in fusing develops. Fusing kilns as large as 4' x 8' are not out of the question for those who foresee large scale in their development. The limitations of fusing are only in the mind and certainly not in the kiln.

188. Partlow controller. *Charts the readings by inking the actual temperature related to time. It can be programmed by cutting ⅛-inch Plexiglas in a pattern to make a cam that controls the cycle.*

189. Barber Coleman clock-driven cam controller *on a 24" x 48" top-loading kiln.*

190. Digitry controller. *Push-button programmable instrument that can control five kilns simultaneously, each having a different time-temperature cycle. The temperature is indicated on an LCD readout.*

190

FIRING THE KILN

CHAPTER 11

191

Firing the kiln involves monitoring and controlling the temperature inside the kiln to obtain the desired heating and cooling schedules. Observing the glass in the kiln at its viscous forming stage is a necessary part of this process. In this chapter, we will discuss the steps involved in achieving successful firings. Record-keeping (graphs) of actual firings are illustrated. Understanding the procedures in this section will enable you to achieve and repeat successful firings. *The principles of firing are the same for all glasses and all kilns.*

191. Bullseye/Marathon *(20" x 20") kiln with front-loading door removed during the rapid cooling stage of the fusing cycle. This kiln, used at Bullseye Glass Company to conduct daily compatibility tests for sheet glass production, is equipped with a Partlow controller.*

Kiln Firing Procedure

No finger marks

1. Prepare the shelf with shelf primer. Place the cleaned glass work on the shelf, and put the shelf into the kiln. (See Chapter 4.)

2. Place the cone in the kiln sitter if the kiln is so equipped; if not, set a timer as a reminder that the kiln is on, or note the starting time.

3. Set up your firing record. Take thorough and accurate notes during firing, recording such information as when closing the lid or changing switch settings. All firing records should be accompanied by drawings or actual patterns of the projects, with glass descriptions and the manufacturer's glass number noted on the drawings.

4. Close the door; prop it open 1/2" to vent if any organic materials are present. Surface frosting is often caused by insufficient venting of the kiln at the beginning of the firing process. Overglazes, liquid gold or palladium lusters, and glue emit fumes during the initial stages of firing. All fumes should escape the kiln before closing the lid.

5. Plug in the kiln; push the kiln sitter button on the outside if so equipped.

6. Pencil in a desired curve on your firing graph as an outline to follow. You will begin controlling the kiln and learn faster if you know what you want the kiln to do.

→ 7. Take out the spacer and close the door (lid) when the kiln temperature reaches approximately 900 degrees F. At this temperature, fumes from any volatile material have been vented from the kiln.

8. Fusing should be completed by the time the kiln temperature reaches 1500 to 1620 degrees F. The kiln sitter will automatically shut the kiln off at 1620 degrees F. using a small cone 011. (This is a good cone to use as a deterrent to overfiring.)

9. Unplug the kiln when fusing is completed, or after annealing if firing down. (See definition in this chapter.)

10. Do not open the kiln more than 1/2" to vent until the temperature has dropped to 200 degrees F.

Cone 16   1517°F
Cone 15   1549°F
Cone 14   1596°F
Cone 13   1615°F

Record-keeping and Firing Graphs

We have mentioned record-keeping throughout this book; however, we cannot over emphasize how important good records are to successful fusing. The graphs in this chapter show how records are kept at the Fusing Ranch. These records indicate all settings used when firing and annealing (firing down) with each of the three kilns described in Chapter 10. To assist in setting up your own records, a full-sized blank graph has been included in the Appendix for you to reproduce. It is most important to note the infinite switch settings through the complete firing and annealing cycles. It is these settings which will enable you to reproduce your results.

If shelf space is available, place a clear base glass of equal thickness to your project in each kiln firing. If any stress exists due to annealing, it can be observed on the Stressometer. Once you are assured that your firing schedule is producing properly annealed results, you may dispense with this test.

If you do not use one of the kilns described in Chapter 10, determine your firing schedule by following the temperature curves on the graphs in this chapter. It is possible to fire any kiln with this basic understanding. Remember, side-fired kilns should be fired like the Bullseye/Octagon 16.

Firing the Pinto

The Pinto has the advantage of a naturally slow heat-up since it is a 110-volt/14-amp kiln; thus it has less power than do other kilns mentioned in this book. With the elements in the top of the lid, heat is uniformly distributed over the 13" circular shelf, and firing becomes simple. Place the glass in the kiln, and turn the temperature control switch to "high." Graph 194 shows the result of a fire-up-to-fuse followed by a natural cool. No venting was used, and a sufficient anneal cool curve resulted for glasses 1/4" and thinner. A lower temperature setting (to #4) would be used for 30 minutes before turning to "high" if slumping or re-firing a previously fused piece. After this slower initial heat-up, the Pinto temperature control switch could then be turned to "high."

When annealing glass pieces thicker than 1/4", the kiln should be turned back on to setting #1 when the thermocouple reads 900 degrees F., thereby slowing the anneal cool at the proper glass temperature. (See "Firing Down" in this chapter.) As you will note on the Pinto graph, the glass would be at 950 degrees F. The Pinto firing graph shows the readings of four thermocouples: #1 was placed under the shelf, #2 was the controlling thermocouple (and came equipped with the kiln), #3 was placed between the glass and the shelf, and #4 was resting on the glass. This test was performed to determine the relationship between the glass temperature during the fire-up and cool-down cycles and the thermocouple readings. *This relationship will be similar for all firings and all kilns when using a clay or mullite shelf.*

Firing the Bullseye/Octagon 16 and Other Side-Fired Kilns

Graph 195 shows the firing schedule for the Bullseye/Octagon 16 with one shelf placed one inch above the kiln floor. This kiln is 9 inches deep and is often fired with two shelves. If one shelf is placed one inch from the bottom and the second shelf is stilted four inches higher, an even firing of both will result. This graph indicates the settings and the temperature rise when this kiln is fired with two shelves.

With tall kilns, you will have to experiment with different stilt heights to obtain the same heat soak on each shelf. It is difficult to achieve equal fusing results with more than two shelves because the heat gradient from top to bottom is usually more than 25 degrees F. in any tall kiln. Because heat rises, the top of the kiln will be hotter. Therefore, it is apparent that the glass on the top shelf will mature before the glass on the lower shelf. By experimenting with different heat-up rates and shelf locations in tall kilns with multiple heating rings, it is possible to achieve uniform heating throughout a kiln. Nevertheless, each multiple-shelf kiln will pose an individual problem. Accurate record-keeping of specific situations is necessary to successfully fire tall kilns.

In side-fired kilns, the initial heating rate must be slow to avoid cracking due to uneven heating across the diameter of the glass piece. Since the glass closest to the heating elements receives heat before the glass in the center, unequal expansions due to temperature differences will cause cracking.

The larger the diameter of the kiln, the greater the temperature differential in the glass from the outer edge to the center of the kiln shelf. Because of this, it is essential to regulate a slower heat-up to the strain point.

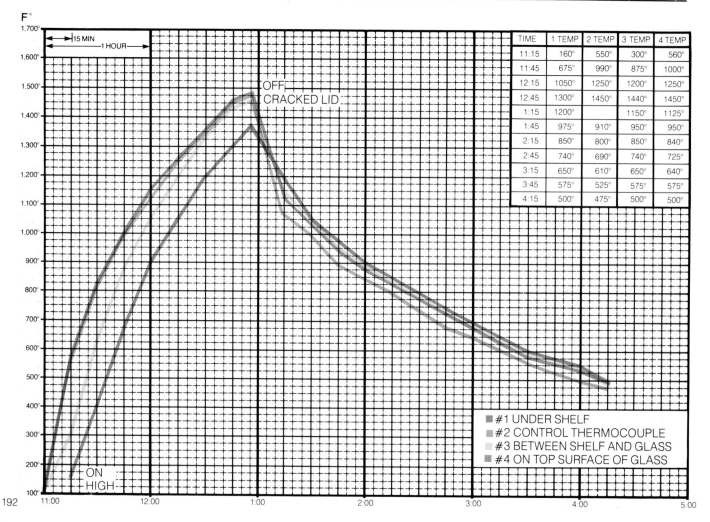

TIME	1 TEMP	2 TEMP	3 TEMP	4 TEMP
11:15	160°	550°	300°	560°
11:45	675°	990°	875°	1000°
12:15	1050°	1250°	1200°	1250°
12:45	1300°	1450°	1440°	1450°
1:15	1200°		1150°	1125°
1:45	975°	910°	950°	950°
2:15	850°	800°	850°	840°
2:45	740°	690°	740°	725°
3:15	650°	610°	650°	640°
3:45	575°	525°	575°	575°
4:15	500°	475°	500°	500°

■ #1 UNDER SHELF
■ #2 CONTROL THERMOCOUPLE
■ #3 BETWEEN SHELF AND GLASS
■ #4 ON TOP SURFACE OF GLASS

192

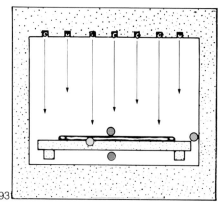

192. Firing schedule for the Pinto kiln. Four thermocouples were read simultaneously. The four differently colored curves represent the various thermocouple readings as noted on the graph.

The Bullseye/Octagon 16 kiln is designed with a kiln sitter as a safety device in case of overfiring, or as an automatic shut-off device if using the cone method when firing. (See Chapter 6, third technique.) We suggest the cone method of firing for those who produce multiple objects (e.g., sets of dishes) from fused or slumped glass. Keep in mind, however, that the proper adjustment of a kiln sitter and accurate record-keeping are necessary to achieve successful firings repeatedly.

Firing the Bullseye/Marathon 20 x 20 and Other Front-Loaders

The Marathon has the ability to fire to fuse temperatures very rapidly due to the overhead element placement and the amount of power present. Fast firing is simple...just set the temperature control on "high." Watch it closely; within 30 minutes the glass will be molten. Firing the kiln slowly requires more control.

Graph 194 shows settings used for a slow firing of the Bullseye/Marathon. Note that the Marathon has two controls; three settings were used for each. The door was not cracked open during the initial heat-up, but it was cracked open one inch for a quicker cool-down to annealing temperature.

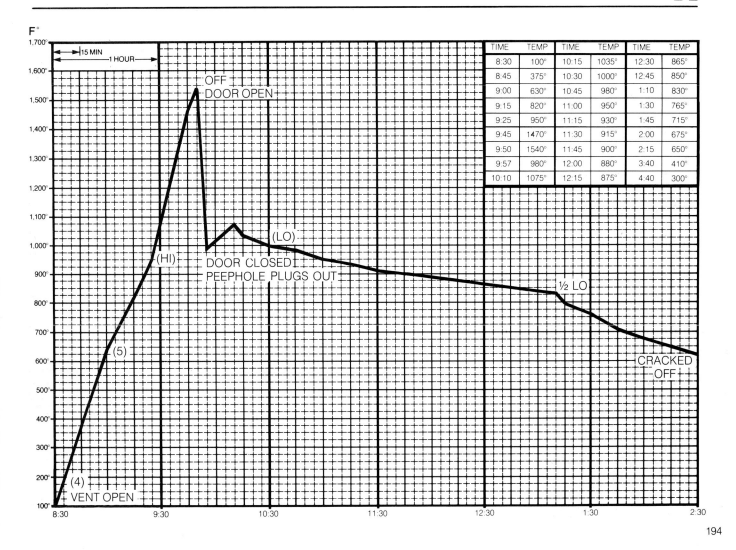

TIME	TEMP	TIME	TEMP	TIME	TEMP
8:30	100°	10:15	1035°	12:30	865°
8:45	375°	10:30	1000°	12:45	850°
9:00	630°	10:45	980°	1:10	830°
9:15	820°	11:00	950°	1:30	765°
9:25	950°	11:15	930°	1:45	715°
9:45	1470°	11:30	915°	2:00	675°
9:50	1540°	11:45	900°	2:15	650°
9:57	980°	12:00	880°	3:40	410°
10:10	1075°	12:15	875°	4:40	300°

194

The Marathon door should not be cracked open for venting; it has two peepholes for this purpose. Because these peepholes are on opposite sides of the kiln and at different heights, they will vent the kiln adequately during the initial heat stage when organic material is present.

Front-loading kilns that are vented by cracking open the door will cause radical temperature differences from front to back; this may cause breaking in the initial heat-up.

Knowing and Controlling Your Kiln

No matter how symmetrically kilns are built, temperature variations will exist within the kiln. Corners are usually cooler, and the top is usually hotter. The configuration and location of the heating elements will determine the heat distribution during firing. (See "Kiln Types," Chapter 10.) Fortunately, nature has an affinity for equalizing temperature imbalances. During cooling, the hot areas give up heat to the cooler areas. This heat transfer is very rapid between two bodies which are very different in temperature, becoming slower as the temperature difference becomes smaller. Because of these temperature differences in kilns, the positioning of glass projects or molds is very important. Molds should be elevated

193. Diagram illustrating the positions of the thermocouples within the kiln which were used to obtain the information for the graph in Figure 192.

194. Firing graph for the Marathon 20" x 20" kiln.

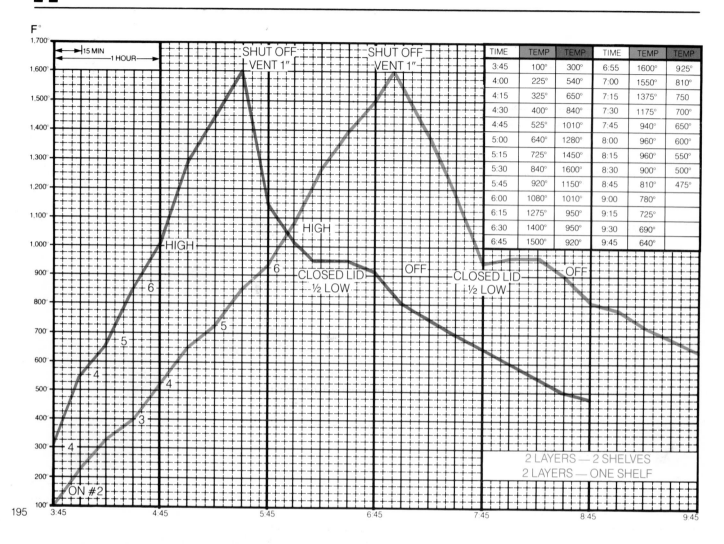

TIME	TEMP	TEMP	TIME	TEMP	TEMP
3:45	100°	300°	6:55	1600°	925°
4:00	225°	540°	7:00	1550°	810°
4:15	325°	650°	7:15	1375°	750
4:30	400°	840°	7:30	1175°	700°
4:45	525°	1010°	7:45	940°	650°
5:00	640°	1280°	8:00	960°	600°
5:15	725°	1450°	8:15	960°	550°
5:30	840°	1600°	8:30	900°	500°
5:45	920°	1150°	8:45	810°	475°
6:00	1080°	1010°	9:00	780°	
6:15	1275°	950°	9:15	725°	
6:30	1400°	950°	9:30	690°	
6:45	1500°	920°	9:45	640°	

195

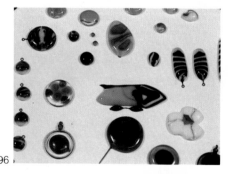

196

195. Firing graph for the Bullseye/Octagon 16" showing the firing curves for one shelf and two shelves.

196. Jewelry projects fired in the Bullseye/Octagon 16". These beginning glass projects were fired according to the graphs in Figure 195.

from the bottom of the kiln, and projects should be centered. The larger the kiln, the greater the heat variation.

The firing stage which requires the most uniform heat distribution is through the annealing range. During the anneal soak process, the temperature of the various components inside the kiln and the temperature of the fused piece are equalizing. When venting the kiln from 1600 degrees F. to 1000 degrees F., temperature differences equalize to within 100 degrees very quickly. However after this point, the heat transfer rate is slower, requiring a soak time and a slower cooling rate in order to maintain temperature uniformity.

It is very important to know what the pyrometer reading actually represents. The pyrometer is used to detect the temperature changes within the kiln. *The pyrometer will give ONLY the temperature reading at the thermocouple junction, not the average temperature of the kiln or the temperature of a piece of glass.*

The rate of temperature change is similar for a point one inch from the kiln walls and for a point in the center of the kiln. Under usual conditions, glass will be changing in temperature at the same rate as the thermocouple. The only difference is that the glass is not at the same temperature as the thermocouple. In other words, if the thermocouple is dropping in temperature from 1000 degrees F. to 800 degrees F. at a rate of 5 degrees/minute, the temperature of the glass is also dropping at the rate of 5 degrees/minute. However, *the glass is approximately 50 degrees hotter than the thermocouple.* (Refer to "Pinto Firing Schedule," showing relative glass temperature compared to the thermocouple reading.)

Since the development of permanent stress in glass is avoided only in the anneal cool range, we should concern ourselves with the glass temperature, not the thermocouple temperature. For example, if the anneal cool range for Bullseye glass is 950 to 800 degrees F., and the thermocouple one inch from the kiln wall reads 50 degrees cooler than the glass, then annealing would best be performed by cooling slowly from 900 to 750 degrees F. when referring to pyrometer temperature readings.

197

Firing Down

Firing down is a term referring to the addition of a small amount of heat to the kiln as it cools through the annealing zone. This is accomplished by again turning the electricity on, setting the infinite switch to its lowest position once the kiln has cooled to the anneal soak temperature. If, at this setting, the kiln does not cool sufficiently to drop the temperature slowly through the annealing zone, a 1/16" to 1/8" spacer may be used to prop open the door to increase the heat loss. By adjusting both the infinite switch setting and the small door vent, any rate of decline can be achieved. Firing down becomes necessary when annealing thick glass which requires a slower temperature decline than that achieved by the kiln cooling on its own. Firing down can also be accomplished by manually turning the temperature control switch off and on, but this method is tedious and does not result in a smooth cooling curve. (See Chapter 6 for the discussion of other controllers.)

The Kiln-Shelf Myth

Clay and mullite kiln shelves actually draw heat out of the bottom surface of the glass at a rate similar to that of the cooling kiln. When fusing flat on a shelf, the concept that glass cools much more slowly on the bottom side is incorrect unless the shelf is resting directly on the kiln floor. This can be observed graphically. (See Pinto Graph 192.) However, when using an insulation refractory such as marinite for a fusing surface, the bottom of the glass which is next to the insulated surface cools much more slowly. In this case, either more soak time or firing down will be necessary. If fiber molds are used, care must be taken to avoid cracking the kiln shelf. If a large area of the shelf is covered by the fiber, the heat difference between the covered and uncovered areas will cause the shelf to break!

When and How a Kiln May Be Opened During Firing

The peephole plug of a kiln may always be taken out for observation. To provide enough light to see, a flashlight must be used at temperatures below 1000 degrees F. Visually, 1000 degrees F. is a dull red heat; above this temperature, the red glow provides enough light to see into the kiln. If only one peephole exists in your kiln, there should be very little perceptible heat leaving the peephole; however, if there are two peepholes and both plugs are left out, one will cause a drafting of the other, allowing enough heat escape to burn you. Be sure to check the amount of heat leaving the observation point with your hand before moving your face too close!

197. *Checking heat with hand before using the peephole as an observation point.*

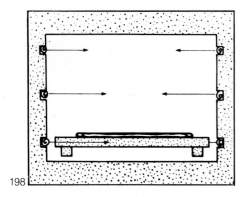

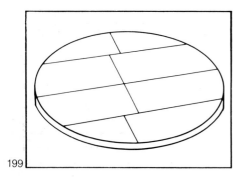

As a general rule, the lid or top of your fusing kiln should not be opened below 1000 degrees F. except when cracked open to vent fumes on the start-up fire. During this venting the heat escape is limited and constant, so it will not heat-shock the glass being fired. The strain point of most glasses will be reached in the temperature range from 600 to 800 degrees F. At the strain point, glass is very susceptible to cracking by thermal shock if the kiln door (lid) is opened too far.

Above 1000 degrees F., the kiln door may be cracked open far enough to make an observation (usually about 5-6 inches). The operator should wear asbestos or other high-temperature gloves. Opening the door for observation will allow a great deal of heat to escape; if this is done too often, the firing time to full fuse will be greatly lengthened. A good indication of which observations will be possible at various temperatures is charted in Chapter 6 (see "The Properties of Glass During Firing"). The peephole plug should be removed prior to opening or closing the lid, because the increased pressure inside the kiln caused by closing will stir up dust. In general, most observations to check the desired fused condition are made toward the top end temperature of any firing.

Solving the Problem of Breakage During Initial Heat

If breaking occurs, there are two procedures that may alleviate the problem: 1) Lower the kiln shelf so that the majority of the elements in the kiln are above both the shelf and the glass (i.e., the shelf is one inch above the floor). This will effectively create a situation of top-firing. It is often said that glass can see heat. This means that radiant heat comes into play, and the glass is being heated before the shelf that holds it. 2) Cut the full glass blanks into halves or thirds before arranging your design on the shelf. This will effectively change the amount of stress created by heat differential. In other words, the smaller the piece of glass, the less thermal gradient is possible across the piece of glass. In the case of a circular piece of glass, the break (due to thermal shock) is usually pie-shaped, separating from the middle and sending pieces outward. By cutting the circle in half and placing it back together, only half the thermal gradient is possible because the distance across the piece is half as great.

When firing more than one shelf of glass in a side-fired kiln, a slow heat-up rate to approximately 800 degrees F. is the only way to insure against thermal shock fracturing. If breaking occurs in a top-fired kiln, slow down the firing.

Irregularities on the edge of a piece of glass may start very small fractures which run and become larger during firing. Check the edges of your larger glass blanks before firing if you think this may be a problem.

198. *To prevent breakage in the initial heat-up, this illustration shows the proper placement of a single shelf in a side-fired kiln.*

199. *Illustration showing a pre-cut blank which was divided into smaller pieces to avoid cracking during the initial heat-up.*

SAGGING, SLUMPING, AND MOLDS CHAPTER 12

Fusing goes hand-in-hand with other processes (e.g., sagging, slumping, molding, draping, bending, and forming). These terms are *similar* in meaning and are often used interchangeably, leading to confusion. Because words are tools of communication, clarification of specific terms used in this chapter is necessary.

Slumping

Slumping is nearly synonymous with sagging; however, slumping usually implies a bending *without noticeable change* in the thickness of the cross section. By keeping the temperature as close as possible to the fiber-softening point (but high enough to allow downward movement), noticeable stretching is avoided. Ruth Brockmann's masks were slumped over a mold, whereas Frances Higgins' Vase (see Figure15., drop-out form) was sagged through a clay ring.

Sagging

Sagging is the downward sinking of glass caused by its own unsupported weight as the glass softens when heated. In glass practices, we refer to sagging as a process whereby the thickness of the cross section of the glass, while being heated, *changes noticeably* due to stretching.

Bending

Bending is a familiar term that does not distinguish between either sagging or slumping. Bending is the physical result of either. Bending, in industry, is *slumping with added weight* applied to the glass, causing the glass to move before it otherwise would by means of gravity alone. Bending takes place much closer to the fiber-softening point than does slumping. Automobile windshields and curved architectural glass are produced by this bending technique to prevent surface marks or cross-section thickness changes in the glass.

Molds

A mold is any object, with a fixed pattern or contour, around or within which another object is formed. It is important to note that in the sagging or slumping process, the mold accompanies the glass through all stages of the firing cycle. All molds used for slumping and sagging must be made from materials which are able to withstand high temperatures. The properties of the mold material give each mold individual characteristics. These characteristics should be given consideration, depending upon the intended use and the desired results.

The permanence of a mold is important to provide time- and cost-effectiveness. Properties such as strength, thickness, and density will determine the durability of the mold. The quality of the mold surface and its ability to retain fine detail will determine the quality of the finished glass surface which was in contact with the mold. Ease of construction and availability of mold materials should also be taken into consideration. As in any endeavor, great satisfaction is gained by maintaining control through completion of the process; however, it is important to remember that the use of a mold (rather than its creation) is the primary consideration. Mold-making is a time-consuming art, and the effort expended may be well worth the creative venture. The ability to make molds allows greater freedom in producing individual and unique glass forms.

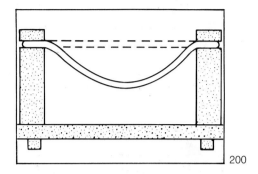

200

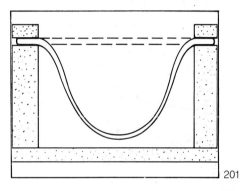

201

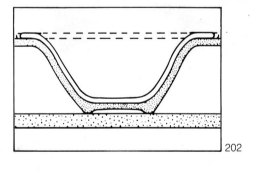

202

200. Diagram showing the cross section of a slumped piece of glass.

201. Diagram showing the cross section of a sagged piece of glass.

202. Illustration showing the cross section of a piece of glass, fully slumped into a mold.

Clay Molds

Clay is an exciting and easily formed material used for mold-making. All clays are acceptable for use as molds; however, some will produce better results than others. Moist, pre-mixed stoneware clay is preferred to low-fire clays. Stoneware is a high-fire clay that matures at approximately 2200 degrees F. It is available in white, buff, and red, but color choice does not affect usage. Simply ask for stoneware at your local ceramic shop, and you will have an excellent mold-making material. Stoneware clays form porous and very durable molds when fired to low bisque temperatures (1600 to 1800 degrees F.). With proper care, stoneware molds are long-lasting. Low-fire clays fired to the same temperatures will be more fragile.

One disadvantage of clay molds is the great change in volume which occurs during heating and/or cooling at approximately 1050 degrees F. (known as quartz inversion). To avoid cracking the mold, the heating or cooling rate should be slow around the quartz inversion temperature.

Forming Clay Molds

Clay can be formed either over or into objects. It is easy to carve or press designs into soft, workable clay. Clay is one of the most versatile of all moldable materials. It can be slip-cast, rolled into sheets, thrown on a potter's wheel, or simply hand-formed.

When the clay mold is complete, four required steps remain: 1) remove any undercuts (areas where glass will flow under the edge and adhere to the mold); 2) air- or sun-dry the clay; 3) fire to 1600 degrees F. (in the fusing oven); and 4) apply a liberal coat of shelf primer or other high-fire kiln wash after firing. A fresh coat of wash is not necessary after each slumping unless the surface of the mold has been scratched or gouged.

If an open, porous clay body is used, clay molds will take less time to construct and dry. The combination of 2 parts clay and 1 part chopped fiber by volume will create a very open, workable mold material. The addition of fiber to clay will also sufficiently reduce the shrinkage so the clay can be sun-dried or kiln-dried at 200 degrees F. without warping. Beyond these suggestions, there is a vast amount of information available at any local ceramic shop on molding, hand-building, and slabbing clay.

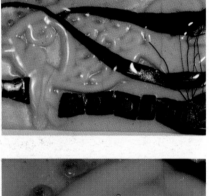

203

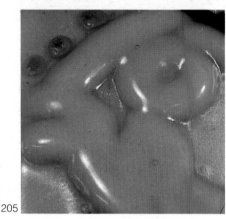

204

205

203. *Various bisqueware clay molds.*

204. *Gail Davis. Fish tile, 8" x 12". This piece was made by sagging the glass over a handmade clay fish form.*

205. *Detail of fish tile from Figure 204.*

206. *Fused bowls askew in their slumping molds after the firing process.*

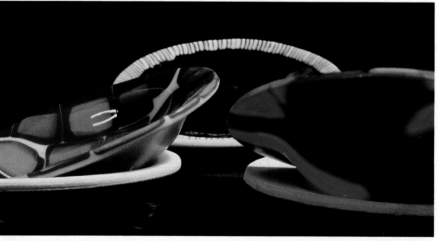

206

Fiber Molds

In the early 1970's, alumina fiber products became readily available through refractory supply companies. Johns-Manville, Carborundum Corporation, and Combustion Engineering are three companies that manufacture fiber products. These alumina fiber materials are generally used to insulate high-temperature kilns.

The molding of fiber blankets is done after a binder and rigidizer have been added to the fiber. Commercial air-setting, moldable fiber is available under various names: Moist Pack, Wet Felt, Moldable Fiber, and others.

Colloidal silica and sodium silicate are two liquids used to impregnate the fiber. The alumina fiber is soaked in colloidal silica and is then compressed to remove excess liquid. Once this has been completed, the fiber is ready to mold over or into a pre-formed object. The wet felt material will then air-dry, retaining the shape of the mold. This process will generally reduce the alumina blanket to half of its original thickness.

The making of moldable fiber should be processed in large batches due to the mess involved and the quantities necessary to produce the material economically. Pre-made moist packs are available through the above-mentioned companies and the Fusing Ranch. This material may be stored in a sealed plastic bag or other airtight container. It will have a long shelf life if it is kept from drying out.

Fiber Mold Applications

The advantages of fiber molds are many and varied, depending upon the scope of the project. The low shrinkage of fiber, the ease in forming large objects, and the great durability are the main advantages of using fiber.

1. Moist-pack fiber can be cut with a razor blade or scissors.

2. Fiber molds shrink less than 2% during the initial drying process.

3. After the initial firing, finished fiber molds may be surfaced with a sanding filler if a finely detailed or very smooth surface is desired.

4. Fiber molds are porous and require vent holes only in the deepest mold cavities. Holes can easily be drilled after the fiber has become rigid. The fiber-mold shapes may also be easily altered by carving away material, or by adding more wet felt and repeating the initial steps.

207

208

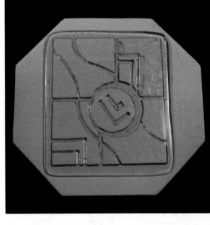

209

210

207. *Fused glass pieces sagged through a rigidized fiber form.*

208. *Fused glass trays made by sagging through a rigidized fiber rectangle.*

209. *Clear glass slumped over a fiber cut-out form.*

210. *Removing the fiber cut-out forms from the slumped piece in Figure 209.*

211

212

212a

5. Fiber molds are durable in the firing cycle and may be used many times if handled and stored carefully.

Making a Fiber Mold

Moist fiber does not dry quickly, so time is not a crucial factor in forming as it is with plaster. The fiber may be cut before forming or after the fiber has dried and hardened. Since moist-pack fiber will stick to most surfaces, a release agent must be used. A solution of 50% liquid soap and 50% water can be applied with a brush over non-porous surfaces. Two applications using a greater ratio of soap to water should be used over bisqueware or other porous materials. Plastic wrap (Saran Wrap™) may be formed over or into an object before the fiber is applied, serving as a release. Aluminum foil works well over very porous objects (such as wood), or when forming over a variety of small objects. When using aluminum foil, apply soap or petroleum jelly (Vaseline™) before laying out moist fiber. Place the moist fiber over the prepared form, and compress the fiber with a smooth object. A heavy glass or rubber kitchen spatula works well. The fiber will air-dry in approximately two days; it should then be removed from the form and fired to 1200 degrees F. before finishing. Faster drying will not create a problem. The fiber mold may be set in the sun or placed in the kiln at approximately 300 degrees F., greatly reducing the drying time. The larger and thicker the mold, the more time will be required for it to dry thoroughly.

Finishing the Fiber Mold

After the mold has completely dried, become rigid, and been fired once, it may be used for slumping. No shelf primer or mold separator is necessary, but the surface will be rough. For a smoother surface, paint the mold with shelf primer, allow to dry, and sand. A mold paste may then be applied to create a very fine surface. Mold paste is made by using 1 part colloidal silica and 2 parts shelf primer. This thick paste will permit fine carving or grinding of the surface, or finish-sanding to a very flat, regular surface. Prepared mold paste is available from the Fusing Ranch.

Large fiber molds should be reinforced with additional layers of moist pack fiber. Since the fiber will not stick to itself, a binder must be used. Fiber binders are commercially available, or they may be made by mixing 1 part sodium silicate, 1 part colloidal silica, and 2 parts shelf primer. This mix can be thinned with water if necessary.

Sodium silicate may be painted on the backside of the mold to make it more rigid, but this material will also make the surface denser and more brittle. Sodium silicate is not appropriate for use on mold surfaces which will be in contact with glass.

Chopped fiber may be added to plaster mixes, clay bodies, or refractory cement mixes, making the resultant mold stronger and more porous. Because ceramic fibers withstand high temperatures and thermal shock, the combination of these materials will increase the durability of the mold. Since ceramic fibers are a new and versatile material, their potential has yet to be fully developed, leaving much room for exploration and creativity.

211. Making a fiber mold from ½" moist pack fiber by forming it over a found object.

212. Completing the mold in Figure 211.

212a. Ma Anand Rupama. Untitled. Finished slumped glass piece made from the mold pictured in Figure 212.

Cement Molds

A castable refractory such as A.P. Green Kast-O-Lite is a suitable mold material; however, it is expensive and no more durable as a mold than a homemade castable using high-temperature calcium aluminate cement.

Producing your own cement mixes is very much like making plaster mixes. Experience and a general understanding of how the materials work together are more important than the 'recipe' used.

Homemade Refractory Castables

Mix by volume:

6 parts calcium aluminate cement (Fondu)
3 parts sand or grog (60 mesh)
2 parts vermiculite
1 part vermiculite (fine)
    (fire clay may be substituted)

The strength of these mixes is most dependent upon the water/cement ratio. Therefore, only enough water to render the mix workable should be added. When testing for proper water content, a handful of the mix tossed up one inch into the air a dozen times should form a firm ball. It is too dry if it breaks into pieces; it is too wet if it sags down through the fingers when they are spread apart. Excess water lowers strength and increases time to set.

When casting the mix, the joints of the forms used should be sealed to prevent water loss while the mix is setting (approximately 24 hours). During this 24-hour period, the form should be kept in a cool, moist place. Following the setting time, these castables must be fired for final curing. With the lid vented, slowly bring the kiln temperature to 1000 degrees F. at a rate of 50 degrees/hour, or slower.

213. Scarab mold made from a homemade castable consisting of 2 parts chopped fiber, 2 parts colloidal silica, and 4 parts silica flour.

213

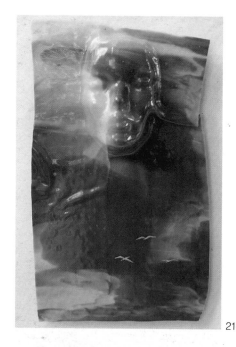

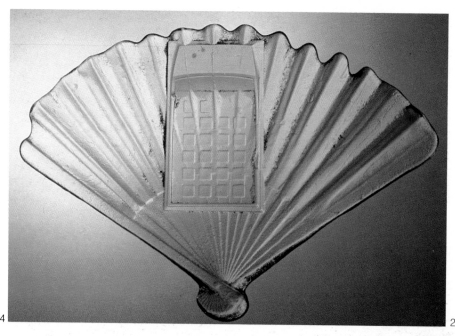

214

215

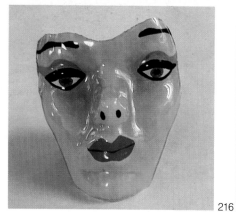

216

217

214. Peter Mangan. *Title: "Sky," 14" x 21"*
A single layer of glass is sagged over a
"durable plaster mix" mold with applied
Versacolor details.

215. Charles Parriott. *Title: "Computer*
Fan," approximately 12" x 12". Clear glass
is sagged over a "one-time plaster mix"
mold.

216. Peter Mangan. *Title: "Wanda," 6" x 8".*
Clear glass is sagged over a "durable
plaster mix" mold. Acrylic paint has been
applied to the screen-etched back
surface.

217. *A single layer of colored glass*
slumped into a commercial dinnerware
plate (see page 94).

218. *Fiber mold cut-out on a prepared*
kiln shelf.

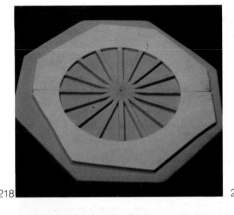

218

219

220

221

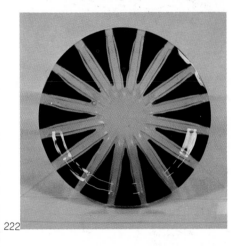

222

223

224

219. Yellow glass blank laid over the fiber cut-out.

220. Pie-shaped, dark blue glass pieces set on the yellow blank between the fiber spokes.

221. Removing the fiber cut-outs after fusing.

222. The completed piece after slumping into a shallow bowl mold. The ribs formed by the fiber cut-outs remain because the slump temperature is not hot enough to cause them to flatten.

223. Fused glass tiles. These tiles were fused on heavily textured fiber with the iridescent side down.

224. Jim Bowman. 6" diameter drop-out form.

225

226

227

228

229

230

231

232

233

234

235

236

Plaster Molds

Plaster molds have been used for many glass-forming processes. The most advantageous use of plaster is not in a permanent mold, but a once-used mold that will easily come apart, allowing for undercuts in the mold. Fine detail is also readily attainable using cast plaster mixes as a mold material.

Plaster of Paris (gypsum), Hydroperm, and Hydrocal are all similar plasters for use in molds. Hydrocal is a U.S.G. plaster which was specially designed for the metal-casting industry. It has more of the desired properties necessary for high temperatures and is the recommended material for the following mixes.

One-time plaster mix is used for molds when undercuts and intaglio design are used. This and all plaster mixes should be cured in the manner described in this chapter's photographic section, "Basic Plaster-Casting Process." One-time plaster can be removed from the finished design with water and a scrub brush.

One-Time Plaster

Measure by volume:

   6 parts plaster

   2 parts silica flour

   2 parts lone grain (80 mesh)

     (80 mesh sand or grog may be substituted)

   3 parts kitty litter

     (vermiculite or fine sawdust may be substituted)

A more permanent mold can be made with plaster, but extreme care must be taken when handling the mold after two or three firings. The greatest problem with plaster is that it continues to break down with successive firings. To his students, Klaus Moje suggests permanently assigning a kiln shelf for each mold, never removing the mold from the shelf. After the mold has cracked (and they will all crack with time), it may be wired together and will remain usable. With this method, kiln shelves could become the most expensive part of mold-making.

Durable Plaster Mix

   6 parts Hydrocal

   2 parts silica flour (200 mesh)

   1 part grog (80 mesh)

   1 part vermiculite (fine), worked through a

     window screen

This mix is more dense than one-time plaster mix and will take longer to dry.

Essentially, plaster mixes can be equated with a concrete mix: the plaster provides the cementing agent; the silica, grog, and lone grain provide a particle size variation for durability and refractory qualities; and vermiculite, kitty litter, pearlite, or sawdust provide porosity. These basic materials may be used in many combinations, depending upon the individual's progressive working knowledge.

Broken molds can be crushed and added to any new mixture in a proportion similar to that of grog and vermiculite. This material, known as "luto," provides a means of recycling leftover mold materials.

225. Make a clay model (e.g., Plastaline-Leisure Clay), avoiding undercuts. (In this example, an overturned saucer was used as a base.) Place the clay model on a piece of glass approximately one inch larger in diameter than the model. Tape a simple box together; the side pieces should be at least one inch wider than the depth of the model.

226. Brush the entire surface of the model and the inside of the box with a 50-50 mix of liquid dish soap and water. Carefully brush out air bubbles.

227. Insert broom straws into the high points of the model to create air-relief holes. As an alternative, holes may be drilled through the mold after casting has been completed.

228. In a dry plastic bucket, mix 6 parts plaster, 3 parts silica, and 1 part kitty litter (vermiculite). The ratio of plaster mix to water is approximately 2:1.

229. Using a container large enough to hold the volume of plaster needed, fill one-third of it with water. Slowly shake the dry plaster mix into the water until the mix floats on the entire surface. At this point, the water will be saturated with plaster and the plaster mix on the surface will remain dry.

230. Mix the plaster and water together until the lumps have dissolved and a creamy consistency develops which coats the hands.

231. Fill the mold with plaster, pouring in a steady stream. While pouring, pound on the table; the vibration created will settle the plaster, level the top surface of the mold, and bring air bubbles to the surface. Blow on the bubbles to pop them. Let the plaster-filled mold sit for approximately one-half hour while the containers are being cleaned.

232. Pull the straws out of the mold.

233. Peel off the tape and disassemble the box.

234. Chamfer or round off all of the outside edges of the mold with a putty knife or scraper to prevent chipping.

235. Carefully remove the clay model from the plaster mold. When the plaster mold has dried sufficiently, any defects can be filled with wet plaster and sanded or formed as desired. Once this has been done, the plaster mold must dry at room temperature for at least two days.

236. After two days, the mold may be placed in the kiln. Set the temperature control to "low" (when using a high/medium/low switch) or number 3 (when using an infinite switch). Hold the kiln temperature at 250 degrees F. for two to three hours with the lid wedged open one inch. Close the lid and fire the kiln to 900 degrees F. Allow the mold to cool in the kiln. Clear the air-relief holes with a thin wire. (Continued on page 94.)

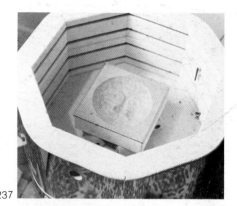

237

238

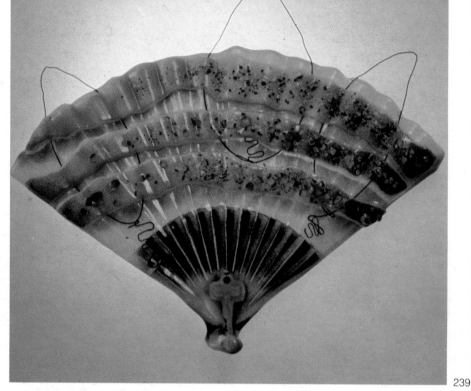

239

237. *Place a glass blank on the mold in the kiln. Wedge the lid open, setting the kiln temperature control on "high" for 45 minutes (or until the kiln temperature reaches 1000 degrees F.). Close the lid. At 1200 degrees F., lower the temperature setting to avoid slumping the glass too quickly. When the temperature reaches 1400 degrees F., slumping should be completed. (Glass may begin to slip in on itself above this temperature.)*

When slumping is completed, turn off the kiln and wedge the lid open one inch for 5 to 10 minutes, lowering the temperature to 950 degrees F. Hold at this temperature for about 10 minutes by gradually lowering the lid. Close the lid, plug the peephole, and allow the kiln to cool to 150 degrees F. (or lower) at its own rate (5 to 8 hours).

238. *Remove the slumped glass from the mold. Trim the excess with a glass cutter and grind the edges as needed. When slumping into a mold for the first time, air may become trapped and will create fine cracks in the plaster. These cracks will help air to escape in future slumpings. If the mold is handled with respect, it should remain usable for 5 to 10 slumpings.*

Found-Object Molds

The Goodwill, Salvation Army, junk stores, and garage sales provide a great source of ready-to-use molds and a resource for ideas and objects for use in mold-making. Metal trivets, bowls, hubcaps, and a myriad of other objects are always available. Plastic and wood objects may be used as forms to shape clay or wet fiber. When taking molds off other objects, wet newspaper, worked over or into the design with a wet sponge, acts as a great release for all mold materials, burning off in the initial firing.

Ceramic dishes or metal objects may be used directly as molds. When using dishes that have already been glazed, care must be taken when applying shelf primer. Roughing the surface of a glazed piece with silica-carbide sandpaper and heating the object in the kiln to 200 degrees F. will allow the glass separator to adhere and dry quickly. If a sandblaster is available, the glaze may be blasted off the surface, making the application of the glass separator much easier. Sand-blasters are also very useful in removing paint or scale from other found objects.

Metal Molds

Metal molds are excellent for sagging or slumping because they provide a highly polished surface and are not susceptible to cracking due to thermal shock or careless handling. Although metal molds are expensive to make, the surfaces can be machined to provide intricate detail. If they are made of iron or mild steel, metal molds tend to oxidize, causing the surface to flake off. Stainless steels are superior to other metals since they do not oxidize. Aluminum is not acceptable as a mold due to its low melting temperature. Cast-iron objects, prepared with shelf primer, may be used for making molds; however, they are inconvenient to use due to their weight.

Thin gauge, spun stainless steel provides an excellent mold for sagging and slumping. Commercially available kitchenware can provide a readily available mold of this type (e.g., an inexpensive, spun-steel wok). All metal molds must be coated with shelf primer. This is best accomplished by using a thicker solution of shelf primer or by heating the metal to 200 degrees F. before applying the shelf primer.

Glass can be formed over or into any metal object. When sagging glass through metal forms (other than contact molds), restraint of some kind must be used to prevent the glass from slipping off the form and falling through the metal shape. Restraint can be achieved by weighting the glass which rests on the metal form (Figures 240 and 241), or by providing enough glass volume, properly placed, to counterbalance the pull of gravity of the sagging portions. (This step must be taken when using any mold of this type, whether or not it is made from metal.)

When making sagged pieces to fit frames for windows, bent-glass furniture cabinets, etc., the restraint method is recommended. All metal which comes in contact with the glass must be coated with shelf primer.

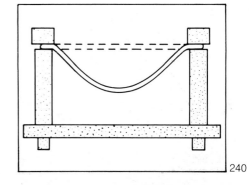
240

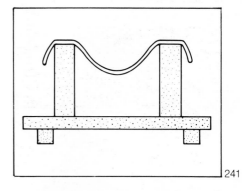
241

General Notes

- In all cases, a mold separator or shelf primer should coat the surfaces of the mold which will be in contact with the glass.
- The primer must be allowed to dry before placing the glass on the mold and firing the piece.
- Steep, vertical sides should be avoided when creating mold shapes.
- Vent holes should be placed at the lowest points within a mold cavity in all but the most porous mold materials.
- Slumping and sagging should be performed slowly, allowing the glass to better conform to the mold.
- Undercuts in high-relief design or intaglio patterns should be avoided (except when using one-time molds).
- Molds should be level *before* firing.
- A rigid mold will not shrink as much as the glass shrinks. This can be a problem when sagging *over* a mold.
- Molds should be slightly elevated from the kiln floor.
- Whenever possible, molds should be uniform in thickness.

Conclusion

Molds add a third dimension to the glass fusing process; they can be as simple or complex as one desires. We hope the information contained in this chapter will provide the stimulus to creatively experiment with molds and their many uses.

239. Dorit Brand. Fused and slumped glass from "Fan Series." Wire inclusions were fused into the fan. The found-object mold was made from a fan and a key.

240. Cross section illustrating the restraint method used in the sagging process.

241. Cross section demonstrating the counter-balance technique used in the sagging process.

13

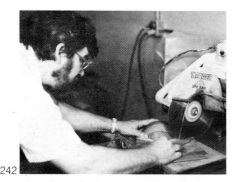

242

243

Saw-Cutting

Sawing can add another dimension to the fusing process. Previously fused pieces can be sawn, shifted, and arranged for re-fusing into a new design. Diamond band saws allow the cutting of tight inside curves and intricate shapes. Klaus Moje's work incorporates saw-cutting in the assembling stages as well as cutting the final fused piece to the desired shape. (See Figure 21.) Diamond sawing is accomplished by abrasive action. The metal blade is impregnated with diamond grains that are harder than glass, thereby providing the abrasive. Diamond saws are available in two types: circular blade saws and band saws.

Circular diamond saws are quite common. Lapidary shops generally stock a variety of models ranging in size and sophistication. The blades are available in various thicknesses and in diameters of 4 to 24 inches. The most common sizes are 6, 10, and 12 inches. A brick or tile saw, available in masonry supply shops, converts to an excellent glass saw by simply replacing the masonry blade with a diamond blade. Diamond-impregnated saw blades are ideal for straight-line cuts and for cutting color bars. The Bullseye Fusing Ranch stocks a 8-inch Gem Saw, recommended as an inexpensive, beginning saw.

Diamond band saws are more expensive but are extremely effective. Their advantage is in the ability to cut curves; their disadvantage is that, for the amount of diamond grains, the blade does not give as much service as the circular blade. The reason for this is that the metal blade fatigues before the diamonds are exhausted; therefore, it is wearing out anytime it is running...even if it is not cutting glass! Gryphon, Denver Glass Machine, and TexSaw are suppliers of diamond band saws. (See "Saws" in 'Glassery'.)

Grinding

The grinding and polishing of fused glass can greatly enhance the appearance of a piece. In some instances, the process can "make the piece." Because glass both reflects and refracts light, the flat, hard-edge quality of ground and polished surfaces interacts with light in an interesting fashion. Bohemian cut crystal is an intricate example of how polished glass surfaces intensify light. The ground and polished edge of a dish or flat shape is a simple example. The difference between a 'funky' piece or a 'quality' piece may be as simple as removing flaws (such as needlepoints) from the outer edge of a plate, or grinding the bottom of a wobbly bowl or platter and polishing it to a fine finish. Grinding can be used as the total design technique, or at various levels, used to enhance or functionalize a piece.

Grinding is the removal of glass by abrasive action. The action of grinding is caused by the wedging of irregularly-shaped grains of abrasive between the moving wheel and the surface of the glass. The glass surface is scratched by the projecting points of the abrasive grains. The larger the grains, the deeper the scratches. As this operation continues, the whole surface becomes covered with an interconnected series of scratches. (Technically speaking, the glass is not scratched, but minutely fractured. See 'Glassery' for details.) Water is used in grinding to increase the grinding rate, to prevent the overheating of the glass, and with bonded grinding wheels, to prevent glazing of the abrasive surface.

Grinding is accomplished in two stages: roughing and finishing. Roughing is performed with an 80-mesh (or courser) grit. Finishing incorporates the use of successively finer grits, starting with 120 mesh and decreasing to a grit as fine as 600 mesh.

242. *Sawing fused glass with a circular diamond saw.*

243. *Sawing fused glass with a diamond band saw.*

244

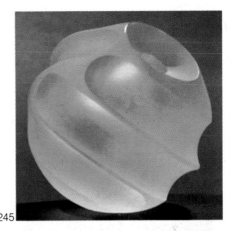

245

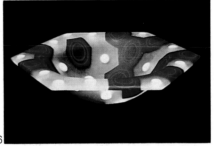

246

247

248

244. Two views of Klaus Moje grinding the inside curve of a fused glass bowl using a glass lathe with a diamond grinding wheel.

245. Clear glass, heavily carved sphere representative of Moje's early work (prior to his involvement in fusing).

246. Klaus Moje. Bowl made by fusing sliced color bars.

247. Various color bars produced by Bullseye Glass Company.

248. A color bar being cut with a Gemstone diamond saw.

249

250

In roughing, actual volume of glass is removed quite quickly. This process is used to obtain the desired shape or size. The finish-grinding process does not remove a significant volume of glass, but rather eliminates the deep 80-mesh scratches by making successively smaller scratches. Depending upon the desired quality of the surface, this is usually executed in three or four stages: 120-mesh grit, 200-mesh grit, and 400-mesh grit (or 600-mesh grit in extreme cases). Once the piece is finish-ground, it is ready to be polished.

Descriptions of Types of Grinding Equipment

Grinding mills are revolving iron plates fed with loose, abrasive grains (such as silicon carbide) and water. The glass surface to be ground is placed on the mill and is moved back and forth slowly across the surface of the revolving plate. When using this type of grinder, it is best to have a separate mill for each grit size used and to separate these mills from each other with curtains. If only one mill is available, all pieces should first be ground with the largest grit; then the mill and the pieces should be carefully washed down, removing all remaining grit. Proceed with the next smaller grit, wash down again, and so on. Obviously, care must be taken to avoid contamination of the grits. For instance, if when polishing with 400 grit, a grain of 120 remained from a prior step and scratched the piece, the whole process would have to be repeated from 120 grit on in order to remove the 120 scratches from the surface. Keep in mind that grits may be recycled, but they will eventually lose their "bite." It is advisable to mix some old, broken-down fine grit with the course roughing grit for better adhesion to the rotating grinding head of the mill. Natural and synthetic stones are available and can replace the cast-iron mill head. These stones may be used instead of the 400- or 600-mesh grit on cast iron.

Belt sanders are excellent for finish-grinding and will also work well for many roughing projects. The beauty of this machine is that only one is needed--it has interchangeable belts of any grit size. As a result, there is no contamination problem! Small, rather inexpensive belt sanders are readily available. We recommend the larger Somaca (3" or 4") for studio work. Belts are available in most cities. (See Figure 251.)

Bonded grinding wheels are used for many purposes and are available in almost any shape and size imaginable. Since various industries use these, they are quite common and are available for use with hand-held electric drills or for specially designed machines. Available wheels include those made from aluminum oxide, silicon carbide, and tungsten carbide. Water must be used to prevent glazing over the abrasive surface. (See Figure 250.)

Diamond-impregnated wheels are metal wheels, saws, and cylindrical drills with diamond grains embedded in their surfaces which work exceptionally well on glass. These tools cut much more quickly than carbides and leave cleaner surfaces. They are expensive, but they are also cost-effective in the long run due to their fast action and durability. (See Figure 249.)

Copper-wheel engraving is one of the oldest and most basic methods of engraving (cutting) art glass. A copper wheel is fed with loose, abrasive grains and water. This method produces a high-quality finish and allows for a very artistic curving technique which requires skill and great patience.

249. Denver Glass beveling machine (left to right): a diamond grinding wheel and a smoothing stone; fiber and felt finishing wheels.

250. Thirty-inch circular grinding mill.

Polishing

This operation is carried out in a manner similar to grinding. Polishing agents occur in a finely powdered form and may be one of three compounds: rouge, cerium oxide, or tin oxide. The polishing agent is applied to a revolving buff made of felt, leather, cork, etc. The action of polishing removes no glass; it merely burnishes the finely scratched surface.

Polishing compounds are used with a minimum of water; thus, great heat is produced from the friction. (Care must be taken to avoid thermal cracking of the glass.) Pumice on a cork wheel is occasionally used as a preliminary polish before using an oxide on felt.

Acid polishing is carried out by dipping the glass in a mixture of hydrofluoric acid and concentrated sulfuric acids. Due to the dangers of working with these acids, it is recommended for only the advanced studio. It is absolutely necessary to have proper handling apparatus and a ventilated hood. There are professional studios that will acid-polish any glass piece. (See "Acid Polishing" in Appendix .)

Fire polishing is accomplished by directing flames or radiant heat onto the glass surface to cause flow. A torch flame is effective for lampworking, but to avoid cracking, requires greater skill for use on thick and larger fused pieces. The following method of polishing edges using kiln heat also works very well. Once the edges of the pieces have been sanded or ground, the edges will fire-polish in a slump firing. Pieces to be slumped should be shaped and sanded prior to slumping, thereby replacing the sometimes tedious cold-polishing phase.

Sandblasting is utilized for producing a diffusing surface on glass articles. By masking areas of the surface, decorative designs are produced. When this operation is carried further, grooves can be cut into the glass and holes drilled through the glass that would otherwise be difficult to produce. Sandblasting is widely used in the flat glass industry, and many books are available on technique and application. *Studio Magazine* (numbers 12 and 18) gives up-to-date information on sandblasting. Many articles written by Dan Fenton discussing various sandblasting methods and the necessary equipment are now being summarized into a booklet form. (See "Sandblasting" in 'Glassery.')

251

251. Somaca belt sander.

14

253

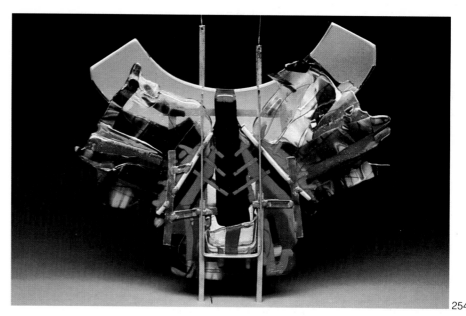

254

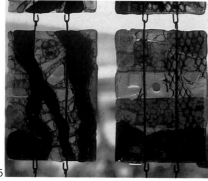

255

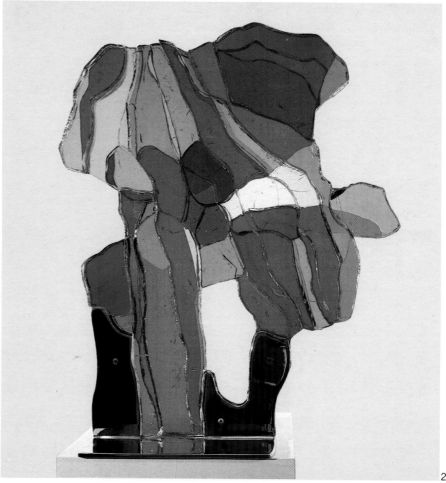

256

253. Jim Bowman. Detail of Figure 254 showing a close-up of the steel hanger.

254. Jim Bowman. "Eagle," 24" x 22", 1982. Fused glass suspended from a hanger constructed of metal bar stock. The metal hanger cradles the fused glass piece, allowing it to be hung from ceiling hooks and viewed from both sides.

255. J. Daniel Strong. Fused glass tiles, 22½" x 22½". The tiles were joined together by hooks and eyelets formed from the wire inclusions which were fused into the glass.

256. Frederick Heidel. "Preposterous Bloom," 34¼" x 25" x 3", 1982. Colored sheet glass and fire-polished plate glass laminated with glue. (See Figures on page 102 for details of metal base).

FINISHING FOR DISPLAY

CHAPTER 14

The display of any finished art work may greatly affect its reception. In creating fused glass objects for display, the desired end or eventual use should be conceptualized as part of the initial design. Depending upon the artist's intention, finishing for display may entail cutting, grinding, polishing, sandblasting, drilling, painting, and/or gluing display materials or other elements to the piece. It is important that means of display not compete with the glass design or otherwise alter the "statement" or "look" of the finished piece.

Hanging, Wall-Mounting, and Framing

Pieces which are to be hung on a wall may be displayed in many ways, each method lending individual character to the piece. Wires may be fused into the piece to form loops for hanging. As an alternative, holes may be created in the design or drilled into the finished piece; eyelets, fasteners, and other "hooks" may be glued to the piece.

Wall-mounting a finished work can be accomplished by gluing a block of wood, metal, or plastic to the back, holding the piece away from the wall to create a shadow-box effect. This method of display will allow some light to bounce off the wall and through the glass, creating depth and a glassier appearance. It is important to back a transparent piece with clear plastic so the mounting material does not detract from the light-transmitting qualities of the glass piece.

Existing door or window frames provide ready-made displays for fused work. When mounting glass in a metal frame, a flexible glue is needed to allow for greater and more rapid expansion of metal in relation to the glass. Transparent silicon glues or similar commercial sealants are best for this use.

Placement and Orientation

Whether the fused object is functional or sculptural in nature, it can be greatly enhanced by proper display. The artist has the opportunity to communicate different feelings in a piece by altering its placement (i.e., its position in relation to the visual level of the viewer) or orientation(e.g., hanging to create the impression of "free-floating" or suspension). Display allows the artist, to some extent, to control what is visually communicated to the viewer, perhaps greatly influencing how the piece is perceived in the environment.

The photographs in this chapter illustrate some of the many and varied ways fused glass may be displayed.

258

257

257. Charles Parriott. *"Fictions: For Those Who Have Worked Themselves to Death,"* 1982. A gallery installation composed of pieces which are all approximately 42" long...a good example of the artist's use of careful placement to control the viewer's perception of the work.

258. Ronnie Wolf. *"Girl Hits Slug,"* 14" x 6" (half cylinder diameter). The piece was designed so the slumped shape would enable the piece to be free standing.

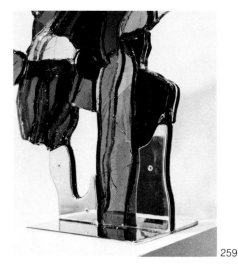

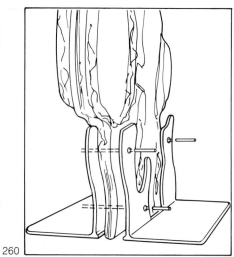

259

260

261

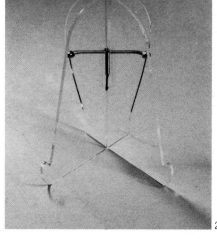

262

263

259. Detail of Figure 256 showing the chrome-plated base (front view). The fabricated metal base (welded ¼" steel) is designed as an integral part of the finished work.

260. Detail of Figure 256 (end view). The glass is sandwiched between the two metal forms.

261. Illustration showing the method of joining the glass to the base in Figure 256. Holes drilled through the glass and metal forms allow flush-mounted chrome-plated allen bolts to secure the base to the glass.

262. A Ruth Brockmann mask in place on a Plexiglas stand.

263. The Plexiglas stand seen in Figure 262, assembled and ready for the placement of the mask. The bar securing the two Plexiglas forms also serves as a wall-hanging device.

264. The components of the Plexiglas stand seen in Figure 262.

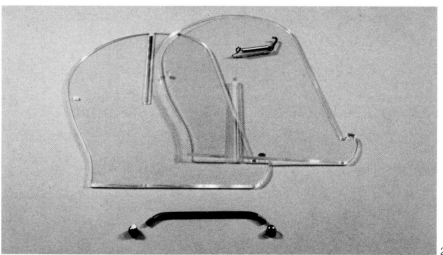

264

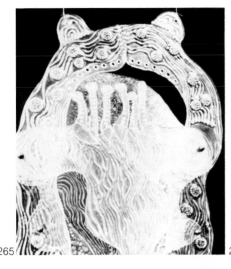

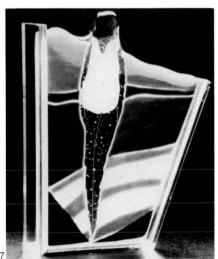
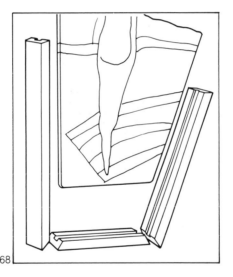

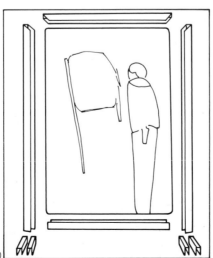

265. David Wright. *Untitled, 10" x 14".* Fused and sagged glass piece designed so that support holes for the nylon line were formed during firing.

266. Ruth Brockmann. *Oval pendant shapes attached to a background. A shadow-box effect is created by the space between the background and the pieces.*

267. Ronnie Wolf. *"Searching," 9" x 9".* Fused glass form held in a free-standing Plexiglas frame. Since the piece is not surrounded completely by the Plexiglas, it acts as a stand and not a frame.

268. Illustration of the stand used in Figure 267.

269. Ronnie Wolf. *"Kiln Watcher," 15" x 10".* Fused glass piece held in a free-standing metal frame made of soldered zinc channel.

270. Illustration showing the method of assembly of the free-standing frame in Figure 269.

271

272

273

274

271. Liz Mapelli. Fused glass tiles, 30" x 30". The tiles were attached to a plywood backboard with silicon glue; no grout was used between the tiles. In this case, the color and texture of the backing material created the visual bridge between the glass components.

272. Detail of Figure 271.

273. Ray Ahlgren. Fused glass tiles, 20" x 36". Three tiles were glued to a framed plywood backing and grouted with commercial tile grout.

274. Detail of Figure 273 showing grouted joint.

275

276

277

278

279

275. Michael and Frances Higgins. *Glass door panels set in existing door frames and held in place with brass bar stock.*

276. Ray Ahlgren. *Untitled, 20" x 24". Fused glass panel glued to a wooden frame.*

277. Klaus Moje. *Fused glass and metal, approximately 3' x 8'. Fused glass panels are set in a welded metal framework and secured with silicon glue.*

278. Peter Mangan. *"Marilyn Goes to Heaven," 15" x 21", 1983. A fused glass panel with kinetic wings and skirt. The city backdrop is part of the wooden frame construction. The skirt and wings are activated by pulling up on the "lift" bar.*

279. *Same as Figure 278: Marilyn at rest.*

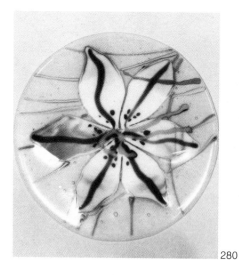

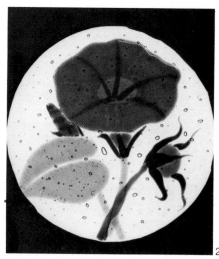

280

281

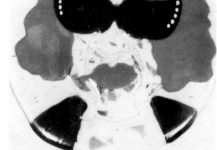

282

283

280. Michael Barton. *6" diameter floral. This simple design is made with frit and stringers that were hand-pulled using a small propane torch. Opalescent glasses were used throughout.*

281. Michael Barton. *6" diameter morning glory with bud. All transparent glasses were used.*

282. Michael Barton. *"Mom," 6" diameter. Fused glass design incorporating iridescent clear glass for the lenses of the eyeglasses; frit was used for the eyeglass frames. Cartoons of these designs are included in the Appendix.*

283. Louise Falls. *"Miami Mom," a variation of "Mom" design by Michael Barton.*

284. Gil Reynolds. *"Punk Mom," a variation of "Mom" design by Michael Barton. A large bubble broke through the glass surface in the nose area; a marble was inserted and held with glue.*

285. David Ruth. *"Black Mom," an abstracted variation of "Mom" design by Michael Barton. (Note: All of these interpretations of one design were created as simple, beginning projects and are ideal for demonstration in a beginning fusing class).*

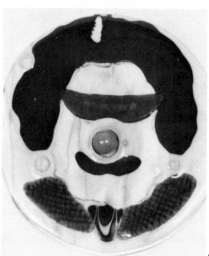

284

285

THE END IS THE BEGINNING CHAPTER 15

The diverse and sophisticated possibilities for the application of glass fusing techniques is already evident in the wealth of work now being produced by contemporary artists. As with the evolution of all art forms, the fused glass movement will continue to develop and mature through the teaching of fusing techniques. Studios, retail shops, and art schools may be a source of valuable information for many prospective students. In writing this book, we have sought to present information that will encourage artists to explore glass fusing and to then share their experiences with others. To this end, an appendix has been provided to supply information regarding classroom instruction and related materials. The 'Glassery' contains expanded definitions of terminology and descriptions of advanced fusing techniques. The photographs in this chapter provide a sampling of further creative ideas for exploration in this exciting and growing art form.

The working of "warm" glass in a kiln-fired mode is exciting from the perspective that the fuser is able to explore glass by working with it in *two* states: molten and cold. Glass may be manipulated in the kiln by employing a variety of techniques including the ancient process of combing and advanced sagging techniques. Iridizing solutions, lusters, and chemicals used to induce blisters can provide many interesting variations by altering the glass surface. Inclusions such as frit or copper wire may further expand design possibilities. In addition, a fused piece may be incorporated into a larger piece by pressing it into an epoxy mix or by gluing it to vitrolite or other materials.

Modern technological advancements have made the age-old process of glass fusing readily accessible to today's artists. The contemporary blown and stained glass movements stimulated interest in glass as an art medium, promoting the availability of materials and encouraging the development of advanced techniques. An important breakthrough was provided by the standardization of testing methods and the development of a commercially available palette of compatible glasses. The ceramics industry was instrumental in furthering the development of lightweight, inexpensive, and easy-to-operate kilns, allowing for greater control of the firing and annealing processes.

While technology and the availability of tools and materials have facilitated the renewed interest in glass fusing, information-sharing is the key to the continued growth of glass fusing. Through this vital exchange of information, glass fusing will surely flourish as a unique and creative art form. Begin!

286

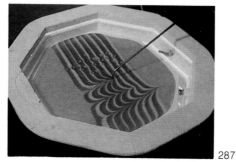

287

288

289

290

286. *The fusing classroom.*

287. *Combing hot fused glass. Combing is a very exciting hot glass technique which can be done in a simple fusing kiln by dragging a pointed metal rod across the surface of the hot glass. (Kiln elements must be turned off when combing glass to prevent electrical shock.)*

288. Diane Kinsey Busacker. *Combed glass bowl, 11½" diameter.*

289. Gil Reynolds. *Detail of leaded glass window. The butterfly is fused glass; the wing pattern was achieved by combing.*

290. Ruth Brockmann. *"Breakfast of Champions," 32½" x 30". Fused glass components are used within a leaded glass window.*

291. *Detail of Figure 290. The Dalmation and the sock are fused glass.*

292. Gail McCarthy. *Untitled, leaded glass window, 18" x 24", 1977. The duck's neck and wings have been sagged and foiled into the window such that the scalloped wings and neck project outward from the piece.*

293. Dorit Brand. *Glass fan form, approximately 12" x 14". Enameled glass is sagged over a wire armature. The protruding wires were wrapped with thread.*

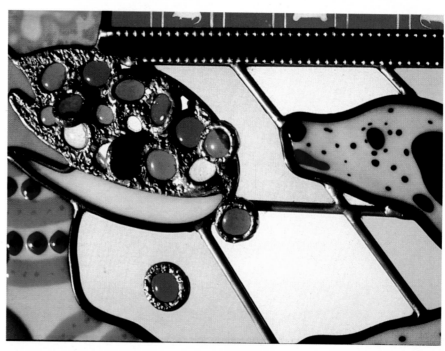

291

292

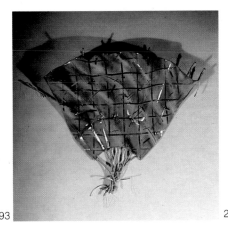

293

294

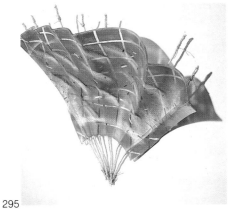

295

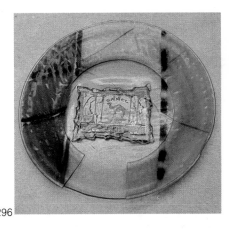

296

297

298

299

294. Detail of Figure 293.

295. Dorit Brand. *Glass fan form, approximately 12" x 14".*

296. Charles Parriott. *Untitled, 11" diameter. An unfolded cigarette package was sandwiched between two layers of glass, fused, and sagged. The high clay content of the paper and the carbon-base ink remain, leaving the imprint of the Camel logo.*

297. A display of advanced fusing technique supplies. Foreground: packaged frit. Center: crucibles for melting glass in a fusing kiln. Background: gloves and steel rod for manipulating hot glass.

298. Glass cane made from glass melted in a fusing kiln.

299. The authors making color bars at Bullseye Glass Company. Gathers of glass are marvered on a metal table and stretched into bars.

300

301

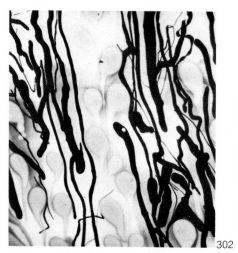

302

303

300. Drips and drools of molten glass which was melted in a small crucible in a fusing kiln. Glass was gathered on a metal rod and randomly dropped onto the floor.

301. An assortment of color bars and drawn cane produced by Bullseye Glass Company.

302. Dale Busacker. "Floor Pickings," 11½" diameter. Detail of glass plate made with free-form drips and drools made previously from hot glass. The free-form lines were laid on a glass blank which was then fused and sagged.

303. Ruth Brockmann. "Cat of Nine Lives," 24" x 24". Detail from a leaded glass window. The outline of the cat is made from included copper wire; the facial features of the cat and other decorations were made with frit and glass stringers.

304. Rick LaLonde forming hot glass lines with a torch. Glass stringers were made by utilizing the thread pull test technique (see Chapter 5) and wrapping the hot glass around a metal form.

305. Glass lines formed by Rick LaLonde as shown in Figure 304.

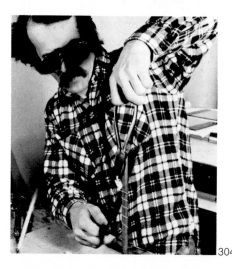

304

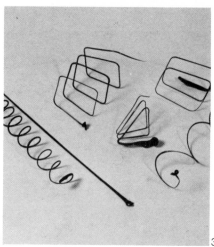

305

307.

306.

306. *Liz Mapelli at the site of the installation of her fused glass tile ceiling in the Portland Justice Center, Portland, Oregon.*

307. *Liz Mapelli experimenting with a lay-up for her fused glass tiles.*

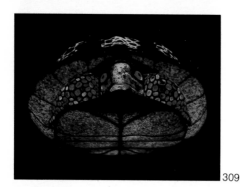

308

309

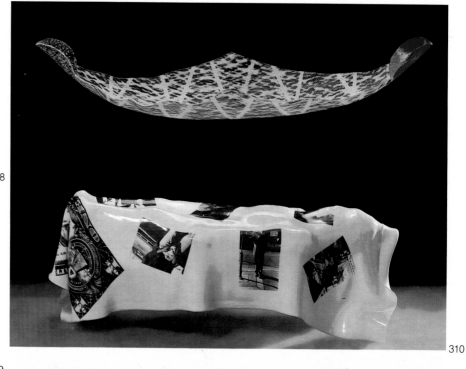

310

311

308. Barry W. Haver. *"Within Without,"* tortoise lamp, 13" x 21" x 26". The lamp is a copper-foiled assembly of fused and slumped glass components.

309. Another view of Figure 308. Life-like detail has been achieved by carefully controlling the patterns in the fused components.

310. Charles Parriott. *"Opposing Fields,"* 43" x 12" x 14", 1982. The shroud form is sagged over a moist pack fiber mold. The images were achieved by the use of decals, fired to the glass surface during the sagging process. The decals were made by a photo silk-screen process from Mark Sullo's photographs. The suspended boat form (40" x 8" x 5") was slumped into a fiber mold. The red tip is fired-on enamel; the geometric pattern was achieved by using tracing black, applied with a carpenter's chalk line.

311. Valerie Arber. *"Dangerous Decadence,"* a gallery installation of approximately thirty fabric-like banners on two twenty-foot ropes. This close-up shows some of the banners which were made by sandblasting flashed glasses and sagging them over metal pipe and kiln-bricks to achieve the flowing form.

CLASSROOM TEACHING

The rebirth of fusing will add depth to the present art glass movement only if teachers of these up-dated techniques first acquire a *thorough* understanding of the processes involved. This book contains all of the information necessary to understand the art of glass fusing. *Working* knowledge, however, can be gained only with actual, hands-on experience. It is our greatest hope that shopowners and other prospective teachers will work with this manual in their own studios for an ample period of time before attempting to teach others.

Fusing is basically simple: compatible glasses are placed on a kiln shelf in a kiln, the temperature of the glass is slowly raised to approximately 1500 degrees F., and the glass is then cooled slowly through the annealing zone. It sounds easy, doesn't it? Yet, exposure to conflicting and inaccurate information may initially create problems for both teachers and students. Fusing instructors may find it difficult to successfully facilitate student comprehension if they have not themselves acquired the experience necessary to correctly respond to questions that are likely to arise in a beginning class. Perhaps if a high standard of teaching competency is maintained in the fusing movement, fewer would-be fusers will be discouraged by the frustrations of initial failure.

Notes to Teachers

• Pre-fired compatible and incompatible sample test strips and a Stressometer are *strongly* recommended for all teachers.

• Blank firing graphs and Firing Schedules for specific projects are to be made available for students.

• Simple, pre-designed projects demonstrating basic color and volume control design techniques should be available for students to complete. It is important that teachers have themselves successfully completed each project at least once.

• A class session dedicated solely to slumping and molds is necessary to allow adequate time for these subjects.

• A two-part slide show is recommended for exposing the novice fuser to student projects and step-by-step procedural instructions for their successful completion; exposure to advanced and professional fused work in part two may provide more stimulating ideas.

• A detailed outline is recommended for use as an educational guide. (See "Outline: Beginning Fusing Class" in Appendix.)

• Those interested in developing teaching skills may attend a course at the Bullseye Fusing Ranch entitled, "Teaching Teachers to Teach."

Notes to Students

• As a prospective student, it is important to be discriminating in class selections, seeking out those that provide valuable supplemental materials.

• It is important that a beginning fusing class cover the basic fundamentals of compatibility, fusing, and annealing.

• Classroom discussions regarding fundamental skills related to the use of necessary equipment to construct fused and laminated tiles, jewelry, and other flat pieces will provide valuable information-sharing.

A Special Note to Shopowners

The best potential market source for the recruitment of prospective fusing students is likely your own mailing lists. These lists may include past customers who completed all the projects they initially intended, or those who did not continue because they had explored traditional glass techniques to their chosen limit. New interest may be sparked in those who became frustrated or discouraged by the intricacies of fitting together and foiling pieces. In fusing, stacking replaces fitting and laborious, cautious planning, allowing the artist to be stimulated by new-found creative freedom!

To assist interested shopowners, the Fusing Ranch offers a three-day fusing workshop. These workshops, hosted by glass shops throughout the country, are taught by trained Ranch-hand instructors at the request of individual shops.

Beginning Fusing Class

This outline may be used for a 6-session/3-hour/day class schedule, or for a 3-session/6-hour/day workshop. Students who work more quickly will have ample time to complete an additional project using an original design. Most important, however, is involving students immediately by providing a satisfying means for them to complete a small scale, quick project during the first meeting. Jewelry or small tiles assure that there will be sufficient kiln space for *all* students to complete an initial project that can be taken home the same day.

I. Hands-On Experience
    A. Making small jewelry pieces and belt buckles
    B. Small tile color combinations
       1. Cleaning the glass
       2. Preparing the kiln shelf
       3. Stacking pieces on the prepared shelf
       4. Loading the shelves into the kiln (turned to "high")
          a. 3-hour class: work will be fused by the end of the class period, but will not be annealed or sufficiently cooled to allow removal from the kiln
          b. 6-hour workshop: work can be worn home

II. Slide Show (Part 1) and Discussion of Prepared Classroom Materials
    A. Full fusing compared to laminating
    B. Opaque designs compared to transparent designs
       1. Overlaying transparent colors
       2. Using clear glass to create depth
    C. Volume control

D. Fused glass designs
   1. Differences in approach
   2. Positive and negative space
   3. Designs without cartoon lines

III. Blackboard Discussion
    A. Testing for compatibility
    B. Testing for proper annealing
    C. Fusing compatibility and annealing overview
       1. Bullseye Stressometer
       2. Pull test
       3. Bar test

IV. Review of Equipment and Supplies (General)
    A. Kilns
       1. Pyrometer adjustments (small cone 019)
       2. Kiln sitters
       3. Firing procedures
    B. Preparing for firing
       1. Shelf primer application
       2. Refractory fiber paper
    C. Additional materials
       1. Gloves
       2. Overglazes

V. Full Fuse Project
    A. Cut and stack a prepared design
    B. Review kiln operation and firing procedures
       1. Firing records
       2. Firing a kiln for the first time

VI. Student-Conducted Tests
    A. Pull test and Stressometer compatibility tests
    B. Devitrification test
       1. Various glasses
       2. Overglazes
    C. Annealing test

VII. Preparation of Second Project
    A. Form working groups of 3 to 4 students
       1. Prepare assigned kiln and shelves
       2. Fire and anneal projects, keeping accurate records for individual projects
    B. Evaluate and compare completed projects

VIII. Slide Show (Part 2) and Advanced Projects for Creative Ideas
    A. History and contemporary fusing
    B. Designing and working in series
    C. Possible fusing directions (discussion)
       1. Using fused glass pieces in windows
       2. Making sets of dishes
       3. Decorative wall and floor tiles
       4. Production work for sales
       5. Fine art

IX. General Discussion
    A. Review previous classroom projects
    B. Present information on additional techniques
       1. Inclusions in glass
          a. Wire and other metals
          b. Bubbles
       2. Fusing upside-down
          a. Low relief
          b. Felt relief
       3. Sagging, slumping, and molds
    C. Discuss future classes

C.		F.
0	32	89.6
0.56	33	91.4
1.11	34	93.2
1.67	35	95.0
2.22	36	96.8
2.78	37	98.6
3.33	38	100.4
3.89	39	102.2
4.44	40	104.0
5.00	41	105.8
5.56	42	107.6
6.11	43	109.4
6.67	44	111.2
7.22	45	113.0
7.78	46	114.8
8.33	47	116.6
8.89	48	118.4
9.44	49	120.2
10.0	50	122.0
10.6	51	123.8
11.1	52	125.6
11.7	53	127.4
12.2	54	129.2
12.8	55	131.0
13.3	56	132.8
13.9	57	134.6
14.4	58	136.4
15.0	59	138.2
15.6	60	140.0
16.1	61	141.8
16.7	62	143.6
17.2	63	145.4
17.8	64	147.2
18.3	65	149.0
18.9	66	150.8
19.4	67	152.6
20.0	68	154.4
20.6	69	156.2
21.1	70	158.0
21.7	71	159.8
22.2	72	161.6
22.8	73	163.4
23.3	74	165.2
23.9	75	167.0
24.4	76	168.8
25.0	77	170.6
25.6	78	172.4
26.1	79	174.2
26.7	80	176.0
27.2	81	177.8
27.8	82	179.6
28.3	83	181.4
28.9	84	183.2

C.		F.
29.4	85	185.0
30.0	86	186.8
30.6	87	188.6
31.1	88	190.4
31.7	89	192.2
32.2	90	194.0
32.8	91	195.8
33.3	92	197.6
33.9	93	199.4
34.4	94	201.2
35.0	95	203.0
35.6	96	204.8
36.1	97	206.6
36.7	98	208.4
37.2	99	210.2
38	100	212
43	110	230
49	120	248
54	130	266
60	140	284
66	150	302
71	160	320
77	170	338
82	180	356
88	190	374
93	200	392
99	210	410
100	212	413
104	220	428
110	230	446
116	240	464
121	250	482
127	260	500
132	270	518
138	280	536
143	290	554
149	300	572
154	310	590
160	320	608
166	330	626
171	340	644
177	350	662
182	360	680
188	370	698
193	380	716
199	390	734
204	400	752
210	410	770
216	420	788
221	430	806
227	440	824
232	450	842
238	460	860

C.		F.
243	470	878
249	480	896
254	490	914
260	500	932
266	510	950
271	520	968
277	530	986
282	540	1004
288	550	1022
293	560	1040
299	570	1058
304	580	1076
310	590	1094
316	600	1112
321	610	1130
327	620	1148
332	630	1166
338	640	1184
343	650	1202
349	660	1220
354	670	1238
360	680	1256
366	690	1274
371	700	1292
377	710	1310
382	720	1328
388	730	1346
393	740	1364
399	750	1382
404	760	1400
410	770	1418
416	780	1436
421	790	1454
427	800	1472
432	810	1490
438	820	1508
443	830	1526
449	840	1544
454	850	1562
460	860	1580
466	870	1598
471	880	1616
477	890	1634
482	900	1652
488	910	1670
493	920	1688
499	930	1706
504	940	1724
510	950	1742
516	960	1760
521	970	1778
527	980	1796
532	990	1814

C.		F.
538	1000	1832
543	1010	1850
549	1020	1868
554	1030	1886
560	1040	1904
566	1050	1922
571	1060	1940
577	1070	1958
582	1080	1976
588	1090	1994
593	1100	2012
599	1110	2030
604	1120	2048
610	1130	2066
616	1140	2084
621	1150	2102
627	1160	2120
632	1170	2138
638	1180	2156
643	1190	2174
649	1200	2192
654	1210	2210
660	1220	2228
666	1230	2246
671	1240	2264
677	1250	2282
682	1260	2300
688	1270	2318
693	1280	2336
699	1290	2354
704	1300	2372
710	1310	2390
716	1320	2408
721	1330	2426
727	1340	2444
732	1350	2462
738	1360	2480
743	1370	2498
749	1380	2516
754	1390	3534
760	1400	2552
766	1410	2570
771	1420	2588
777	1430	2606
782	1440	2624
788	1450	2642
793	1460	2660
799	1470	2678
804	1480	2696
810	1490	2714
816	1500	2732
821	1510	2750
827	1520	2768

C.		F.
832	1530	2786
838	1540	2804
843	1550	2822
849	1560	2840
854	1570	2858
860	1580	2876
866	1590	2894
871	1600	2912
877	1610	2930
882	1620	2948
888	1630	2966
893	1640	2984
899	1650	3002
904	1660	3020
910	1670	3038
916	1680	3056
921	1690	3074
927	1700	3092
932	1710	3110
938	1720	3128
943	1730	3146
949	1740	3164
954	1750	3182
960	1760	3200
966	1770	3218
971	1780	3236
977	1790	3254
982	1800	3272
988	1810	3290
993	1820	3308
999	1830	3326
1004	1840	3344
1010	1850	3362
1016	1860	3380
1021	1870	3398
1027	1880	3416
1032	1890	3434
1038	1900	3452
1043	1910	3470
1049	1920	3488
1054	1930	3506
1060	1940	3524
1066	1950	3542
1071	1960	3560
1077	1970	3578
1082	1980	3596
1088	1990	3614
1093	2000	3632

Prepared fusing projects are the most important tool an instructor can use in the classroom. A fusing project, suitable as a teaching tool, should encompass a minimum of three different forming or layering techniques that are simple, yet strong in concept. The following Michael Barton designs provide the basic criteria for successful beginning designs. All three of these projects help beginning students visualize volume control, frit overlay, stringer or small line detail, and depth construction within a fused piece.

The **Opal Flower** project is laid up on two blanks for volume control. (If this project will not be fully fused to flat, only one bottom blank is necessary.) The flower petals may be made from selected streaky colors and arranged so the surface color shades the inside of the flower. Stringers pulled using a propane torch are laid under the flower to add depth to the

finished piece. Frit and smaller stringers (used for stamen) are added last to create the center of the flower.

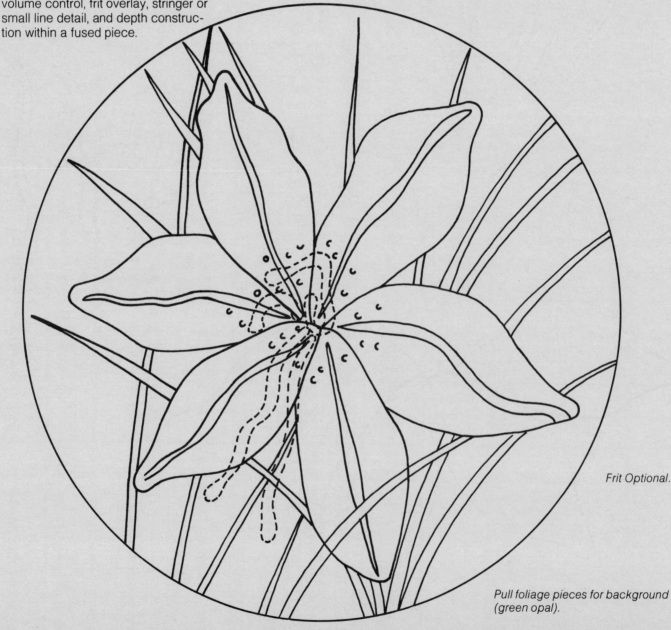

Frit Optional.

Pull foliage pieces for background (green opal).

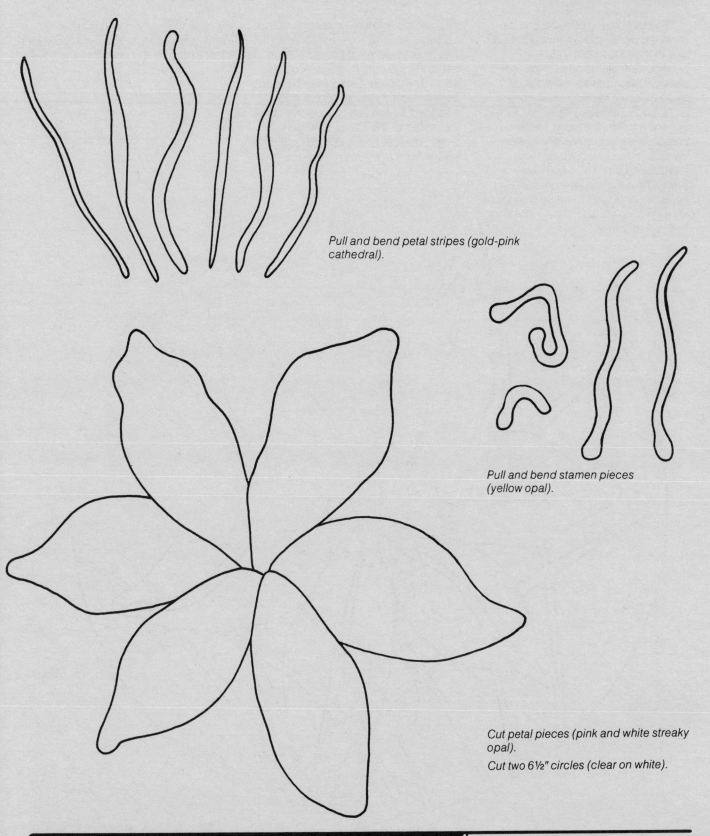

Pull and bend petal stripes (gold-pink cathedral).

Pull and bend stamen pieces (yellow opal).

Cut petal pieces (pink and white streaky opal).

Cut two 6½" circles (clear on white).

APPENDIX

The **Transparent Morning Glory** project uses all transparent glasses and is a particularly useful design because of the number of variations available to the individual student ... nearly every conceivable color may be used! A propane torch may be used to create very controlled flower parts (e.g., sepal). Leaves may overlap the stem (shingled) for dimension, or be set apart (see Figure 280). Petals may be free-formed to some extent and overlapped if additional dimension is desired. When full fusing, this project is set on two bottom blanks.

Flower pieces (gold-pink cathedral).
Leaf (green cathedral).
Pull stems (green cathedral).
Pull bud pieces (dark green cathedral).
Pull flower lines (blue cathedral).
Stamen frit (yellow opal).

Cut two 6½" circles for base plus the flower and leaf pieces below. All other details are pulled and bent lines.

Assemble cut pieces on base and place clear flower center on top of flower piece. Glue pulled and bent lines on top. Add stamen frit pieces, if desired.

APPENDIX

Mom introduces the exciting possibility of portraiture. Greater cutting skills are necessary to produce this design than the two flower projects. Facial features are produced by cutting appropriate streaks from a sheet of pink and white Bullseye #310. Cut-out overlays and frit will add volume to the single-blank background. Small "nibbles" are used for the pearls, and the eyeglasses are made from iridescent #101 clear. If this piece is not fully fused to flat, the eyeglasses will protrude slightly from the background. The volume differential between the eyeglasses (comprised of three layers) and the background (comprised of a single layer) creates depth in the portrait.

Cut a 7" circle of white for base. Assemble face, hair and dress pieces on base. Place glasses and tip of nose on top. Pull and bend eye lines, place on glasses. Cut small squares for pearls, nibble round and put in place. Cut border pieces. Fill background with nibbled frit.

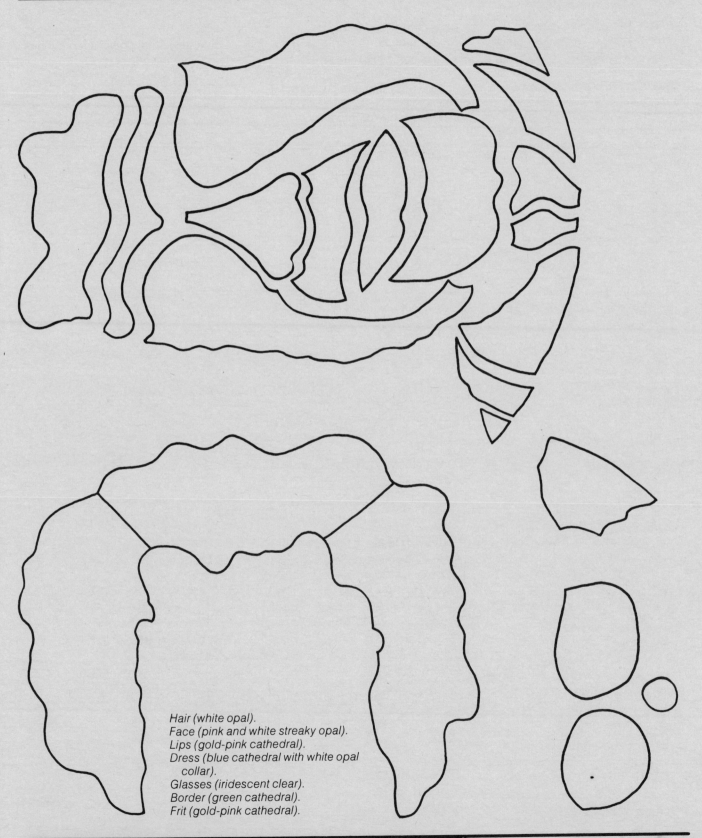

Hair (white opal).
Face (pink and white streaky opal).
Lips (gold-pink cathedral).
Dress (blue cathedral with white opal
    collar).
Glasses (iridescent clear).
Border (green cathedral).
Frit (gold-pink cathedral).

Write or call manufacturers and distributors listed below for product brochures and names of nearest dealers. Check local art, craft, lapidary and ceramic shops, hardware stores, and the yellow pages of the telephone directory for area suppliers.

Acid Polishers/Etchers

Will Hopkins
185 Putnam Avenue
Cambridge, MA 02139
617/354-1977

Pat Patenaude
115 Grand Street
New York, NY 10013
212/925-1140

Art Glass*

Armstrong Glass Company, Inc.
1320 Ellsworth Industrial Drive, N.W.
Atlanta, GA 30318
404/351-3560

Bullseye Glass Company
3722 S.E. 21st Avenue
Portland, OR 97202
503/232-8887

DeSag
Deutsche Spezialglas Ag
Grunenplan
D-3223 Delligsen 2
West Germany
(0 51 87) 77 11

DeSag, c/o Schott American Glass and Scientific Products
3-A O'Dell Plaza
Yonkers, NY 10701
914/968-8900

Merry Go Round Glass Company
8010 Ball Road
Fort Smith, AR 72916
501/646-8001

Oceana Sheet Glass Company
2700 Chanticleer
Santa Cruz, CA 95065
408/476-8457

Spectrum Glass Company, Inc.
P.O. Box 646
Woodinville, WA 98072
206/483-6699

Uroboros Glass Studios, Inc.
1313 S.E. Third Avenue
Portland, OR 97214
503/238-0730

Color Bars

Bullseye Glass Company
3722 S.E. 21st Avenue
Portland, OR 97202
503/232-8887

Houde Glass Company
1177 McCarter Highway
Newark, NJ 07104
201/485-1761

Klaus Kugler Farbglasfabrik
D-8900 Augsburg 21
Postfach 211247
West Germany
(08 21) 3 47 70

Klaus Kugler Farbglasfabrik, c/o C & R Loo, Inc.
P.O. Box 8397
1550 62nd Street
Emeryville, CA 94662
405/658-0771

Zimmermann, c/o S.A. Bendheim Company, Inc.
122 Hudson Street
New York, NY 10013
212/226-6370

Controllers

Barber-Coleman Company
Industrial Instruments Division
1354 Clifford Avenue
P.O. Box 2940
Loves Park, IL 61132
815/877-0241

Digitry Company
Rover Road
Edgecomb, ME 04556
207/633-2638

Honeywell Inc.
Process Control Division MS436TR
1100 Virginia Drive
Fort Washington, PA 19034
215/328-5111

Johnstone Supply
2625 S.E. Raymond Street
Portland, OR 97202
503/234-7221

Partlow Corporation
2 Campion Road
New Hartford, NY 13413
315/797-2222

Enamels

L. Reusche and Company
2-6 Lister Avenue
Newark, NJ 07105
201/589-2040

Thompson Enamels
1539 Old Deerfield Road
P.O. Box 127
Highland Park, IL 60035
312/831-2231

Fiber Products

Carborundum Corporation
Resistant Materials Company
Refractories Division, Dept. TR
P.O. Box 156
Niagara Falls, NY 14302
716/278-2671

Combustion Engineering, Inc.
900 Long Ridge Road
Stamford, CT 06902
203/329-8771

Johns-Manville (Manville Corporation)
12999 Deer Creek Canyon Road
Littleton, CO 80123
303/978-2000

Grinding and Beveling Equipment

Denver Glass Machine, Inc.
1804 South Pearl Street
Denver, CO 80210
303/744-8004

Glastar Corporation
19515 Business Center Drive
Northridge, CA 91324
213/993-5091

*See the Glass Registry and trade magazines for other art glass suppliers.

H. Putsch and Company, Inc.
P.O. Box 5126
Asheville, NC 28803
704/684-0671

Sommer and Maca Industries, Inc.
5501 West Ogden Avenue
Chicago, IL 60650
312/242-2871

Kilns, Fusing

Denver Glass Machinery, Inc.
1804 South Pearl Street
Denver, CO 80210
303/744-8004

Fusing Ranch
3625 S.E. 21st Avenue
Portland, OR 97202
503/232-0776

Glass Fusion Studio (kit)
1618 S.E. Ogden Street
Portland, OR 97202
503/235-2284

Molds

Fusing Ranch
3625 S.E. 21st Avenue
Portland, OR 97202
503/232-0776

Glass Fusion Studio
1618 S.E. Ogden Street
Portland, OR 97202
503/235-2284

Thompson Enamels
1539 Old Deerfield Road
P.O. Box 127
Highland Park, IL 60035
312/831-2231

Plaster

United States Gypsum Plaster
Company
101 South Wacker Drive
Chicago, IL 60606
312/321-4000

Refractories

A.P. Green Refractories Company
Green Boulevard
Mexico, MO 65265
314/473-3626

Carborundum Corporation
Resistant Materials Company
Refractories Division, Dept. TR
P.O. Box 156
Niagara Falls, NY 14302
716/278-2671

C. H. Murphy, Inc.
26 Del Prado
Lake Oswego, OR 97034
503/635-2511

Combustion Engineering, Inc.
900 Long Ridge Road
Stamford, CT 06902
203/329-8771

Saws

Denver Glass Machinery, Inc.
1804 South Pearl Street
Denver, CO 80210
303/744-8004

Fusing Ranch
3625 S.E. 21st Avenue
Portland, OR 97202
503/232-0776

Gemstone Equipment
Manufacturing Company
480 East Easy Street, Building 1
Simi Valley, CA 93065
805/527-6990

Gryphon Corporation
101 East Santa Anita Avenue, Dept. S
Burbank, CA 91502
213/845-7807

Sommer and Maca Industries, Inc.
5501 West Ogden Avenue
Chicago, IL 60650
312/242-2871

TexSaw
P.O. Box 4668
Waco, TX 76705
815/799-2462

Switches

W. W. Grainger, Inc.
Department TR
5959 West Howard Street
Chicago, IL 60648
312/647-8900

Johnstone Supply
2625 S.E. Raymond Street
Portland, OR 97202
503/234-7221

GLASSERY

Acid polishing: .... See **Polishing.** (Also see list of supplies in the Appendix.)

Alumina hydrate: .... ($Al_2O_3 \cdot 3H_2O$) A fine, white powder manufactured from bauxite by the Bayer process; a major ingredient in shelf primer.

Aluminum oxide: .... (Al_2O_3) A crystalline compound used in abrasives and refractories; commonly used for grinding.

Anneal: .... The controlled cooling of glass to achieve the desired final distribution and amount of stress in the glass when it has reached room temperature. The annealing process is made up of two stages: anneal soak and anneal cool. (See Chapter 7.)

Anneal cool: .... The stage in which glass is cooled from the annealing soak temperature to the strain point. This cooling should occur at a rate that is sufficiently slow so that undesired residual stresses will not re-appear when the glass temperature has reached equilibrium.

Annealing point: .... The temperature at which the internal strains in glass are reduced to an acceptable limit in a matter of minutes. For most glasses, the annealing point temperature is 35 to 40 degrees F. above that of the strain point.

Annealing range: .... The temperature range which exists just above the strain point to the anneal soak temperature. The annealing range of a specific glass may be available from the manufacturer, or the glass can be tested to determine the proper temperature range. (See "Testing Glass for Determination of the Annealing Range," Chapter 7.)

Anneal soak: .... The stage in cooling when the glass is held at a constant temperature for a time that is sufficient to relieve existing stress and to stabilize the glass.

Asbestos: .... A fireproof, fibrous material composed of hydrated magnesium silicate. Asbestos gloves are available to protect the wearer from extreme heat when working with hot glass.

Atmosphere: .... The prevailing condition of the air in the kiln during firing. This condition can vary from oxidation (excess of oxygen) to neutral to reduction (deficiency of oxygen).

Base glass: .... The bottom layer of glass, or parent glass, to which other glasses are fused; may also refer to the most frequently used glass in a given fusing project.

Batch: .... The raw material used in the production of glass, properly proportioned and mixed, which is ready for melting in the glass furnace.

Bending: .... The physical result of the sagging or slumping of glass.

Bentonite: .... Either of two principally aluminum silicate clays, containing some magnesium and iron, distinguished by sodium or calcium content with corresponding high or low swelling capacity. Bentonite is used in various adhesives, cements, ceramic fillers, and shelf primer.

Bent glass: .... Sheet glass that has been shaped into three-dimensional form by firing on, within, or over forms. The term, "bent glass," signifies glass that has been slumped with added weight applied to the glass, causing it to move before it otherwise would by means of gravity alone. In this case, bending takes place closer to the softening point than does slumping. Automobile windshields and curved architectural glass are produced by this bending technique to prevent surface marks or cross-section thickness changes in the glass.

GLASSERY

Beveling: .... The grinding and polishing of a glass edge at an angle other than 90-degrees.

Bisque: .... Clay ware that has been fired to a state where it has ceramically bonded but remains very open and porous; not fired to maturity. Bisqueware is often used to make molds for sagging and slumping.

Blank: .... A piece of sheet glass, cut to a predetermined shape and size, used as the base glass on which to lay up fused glass designs.

Blister: .... A relatively large bubble occurring in sheet glass that is often considered to be a desired characteristic in art glass; this same characteristic is considered to be a defect in commercial float glass.

Blown glass: .... Glass that is formed by blowing as opposed to rolling or drawing.

BTU: .... (British Thermal Unit) The quantity of heat necessary to raise one pound of water one degree Fahrenheit.

Calcium carbonate (Whiting): .... ($CaCO_2$) A fine, white powder occurring naturally as chalk, limestone, marble and other forms used in a variety of manufactured products including shelf primer.

Cane: .... Slender glass rods, usually less than ¼" in diameter, such as the color rods used to create millefiore.

Cathedral glass: .... A term applied to transparent colored sheet glass.

Ceramic fiber insulation: .... Material composed of alumina silicate fibers, used in kiln construction. It is very lightweight and absorbs less heat during heat-up than does insulating firebrick, making the kiln operation for fusing more economical.

Ceric oxide: .... (CeO_2) A pale, yellowish-white powder used to polish glass.

Chemical durability: .... The ability to withstand wear or decay as a result of exposure to corrosive materials. Among materials, glass ranks high in the scale of chemical durability, providing products of long utility. When a glass is chemically durable, it does not weather by producing a scummy or foggy surface in acid rain. Chemical durability in glass is determined by its chemical composition. Glasses which have a high boron content exhibit excellent chemical durability. Soda lime glasses with calcium oxide contents above 9% are also chemically durable.

Cloisonne: .... A technique using thin metal wires, usually of gold or silver, which are shaped into a design on a metal base, forming "cells" which are then filled with finely ground enamels and fired to maturity.

Coating cement: .... A substance generally composed of colloidal silica and a fine-particle clay (EPK) commonly used to coat fiber molds and kiln floors. Coating cement is used in place of kiln wash or shelf primer in fiber-insulated kilns to protect the kiln floor in the event of a melt-down, as it effectively hardens the surface, making it resistant to deterioration caused by glass melting into the fiber.

Coefficient of expansion: .... A number indicating the percentage of change in length, per degree Centigrade change in temperature. (See "Coefficients of Expansion," Chapter 5.)

Colloidal silica: .... A suspension of finely divided silica particles in a liquid medium used as a bonding agent in cements.

GLASSERY

Combing: An ancient technique used by Roman glass blowers, which can be directly applied to the fusing process. Different layers of colored glasses are assembled on a kiln shelf. The glasses are heated to well above full-fuse temperatures (1700 degrees F.) until the surface is liquid enough to be moved (combed) with a metal instrument. Design techniques may vary from symmetrical (e.g., feathering) to totally abstract.

A broom handle with a ⅛" metal hook screwed into the end makes an excellent, inexpensive combing device. Drawing a rod across molten glass at 1700 degrees F. is an exciting experience: the glass gives way slowly but consistently, and great volume control can be achieved. As the glass cools, combing becomes more difficult to control. If the glass cools sufficiently before combing is completed, the kiln may be closed, turned back on, and the glass re-heated.

NOTE: Avoid using an all-metal device for combing. By touching an element under power with the combing device, you may receive a powerful and dangerous electric shock! Be sure the kiln temperature control has been turned to OFF and use a wood-handled combing device.

Compatibility: The characteristic of glasses that allows them to be fused together and, after proper cooling to room temperature, have no undue stresses that will lead to fracturing.

Cone: A small, slender, unfired clay pyramid designed to soften and bend at a specific point related to time **and** temperature. The specific ceramic composition is identified by a number that indicates the capacity for heat tolerance before bending.

Cool to room temperature: The cooling stage wherein the temperature of glass is reduced from the strain point to room temperature. This process need only proceed slowly enough to prevent shattering and will depend upon the thickness of the fused piece.

Crazing: A fine network of cracks in the surface of glass.

Crucible: A ceramic pot in which glass can be melted. Common fire clay crucibles are adequate for most fusing studio applications. A more durable crucible can be made by using the following formula:

Alumina	50	
Kaolin clay	20	
Grog (fine)	10	+ 1.5% Bentonite
Grog (course)	10	
Ball clay	10	

Add water to the dry mixture and wedge to a proper throwing consistency. Fire to 2300 degrees F.

Cullet: Scraps of broken or waste glass for re-melting.

Decal: A picture or design printed on special paper for transferring to glass, metal, or other material by the process of decalcomania.

Devitrification: Crystallization in glass, usually occurring as a scum on the surface of the glass. This crystallization takes place when glasses are held at temperatures slightly below the liquidus temperature for each glass; this temperature is approximately 1400 degrees F. for most glasses.

GLASSERY

Double strength glass: .... Clear window glass that is ⅛" thick.

Drawn glass: .... Referred to as "machine antique" glass; resembles blown glass (but is much less expensive). Drawn glass is formed by the vertical pulling or drawing by means of the Fourcault method. This method was, in the past, used in the manufacture of window glass because it produces a sheet which is very uniform in thickness.

Dry strength: .... The strength a material acquires after it has dried, but before it has been fired. With an overglaze, dry strength refers to its capacity to bond to the surface to which it has been applied. This is an especially important property of overglazes because it allows the handling of glass pieces after spray application.

Elasticity: .... The capacity to return to the initial form or state following deformation.

Element: .... A coil of resistance wire through which current passes, creating the necessary heat for firing in an electric kiln.

Enamel: .... A substance composed of finely ground colored or clear glasses which are available as powders or suspensions in liquid media.

Expansion coefficient: .... See **Coefficient of Expansion.**

Fabricut: .... A carbide-impregnated cloth with an open weave that is used to sand shelf primer from a kiln shelf.

Fiber paper: .... An alumina silicate fiber paper that may be used as a fusing surface in place of shelf primer or to provide surface relief. Fiber paper imparts a subtle matte finish to the glass surface.

Fiber softening point: .... The temperature, well above the annealing range, at which glass will deform under its own weight. It is tested by placing an unweighted glass fiber in a special furnace with the temperature increasing at a rate of 5 degrees C./minute. The fiber softening point corresponds to an elongation rate of 1 millimeter/minute.

Firing down: .... The addition of a small amount of heat to the kiln while cooling through the annealing range in order to slow the cooling rate.

Firing schedule: .... The record of time and temperature during the fusing cycle.

Flameware: .... Glass that will not crack when subjected to direct flame at room temperature. See **Pyrex.**

Flashed glass: .... Sheet glass that consists of two distinct layers of glass of different colors; one glass layer is usually thinner than the other. When sandblasted or etched away in varying amounts, shading can be achieved. When flashed glass is fused on top of a third color, the piece will outline itself because of the natural tendency for fused glass edges to turn up.

Float process: .... A process by which all commercial window glass in the U.S.A. is produced. Molten glass is floated over the surface of a bath of molten tin where it spreads out to a sheet of uniform thickness, producing an excellent, fire-polished surface on both sides.

Fire polishing: .... See **Polishing.**

Flux: .... A substance that promotes fusion, or one that aids and induces flow.

Frit: .... A material which consists of a glass that has been melted, cooled, and crushed or ground. Frit is available in a variety of sizes.

GLASSERY

Fugitive: . . . . A term applied to the elusive nature of a material, a color, or a visual effect that is short-lived or difficult to control.

Full-fuse temperature: . . . . The temperature (approximately 1550 to 1620 degrees F.) at which glasses melt together to form a flat surface. (Note: This temperature may vary for different individual glasses.) A hard glass (e.g., plate glass) will fully fuse at 1620 degrees F.; a soft glass (e.g., Spectrum) will fully fuse at 1550 degrees F.

Fuse: . . . . To join together by the application of heat.

Fuse-to-stick: . . . . Fusing at the lowest temperature possible and yet have separate pieces of glass stick together. Glasses retain all of their individual character and the edges round slightly. No noticeable flow or displacement of the individual layers of glass occurs.

Fusing ranch: . . . . A business, associated with Bullseye Glass Company, which supplies materials necessary for fusing art glass.

Galvanometric: . . . . See **Pyrometer.**

Gasket: . . . . Ceramic fiber frequently used as a seal between the kiln and the kiln door to prevent the escape of heat.

Glass blowing: . . . . The art or process of shaping an object from molten glass by blowing air into it through a tube.

Grinding: . . . . The removal of glass by abrasive action. The grinding action is caused by irregular-shaped grains of abrasive material between the moving wheel and the surface of the glass. The glass surface is crushed by the high pressure developed by some projecting point of the abrasive grain which produces a small check in the glass. As this operation continues, the whole surface becomes covered with small checks. The size of these irregularities and the depth of the checks are dependent upon the size of the abrasive grains and their crushing strength.

Water or a suitable cutting fluid is used in grinding to increase the grinding rate, to prevent overheating of the glass, and, with bonded grinding wheels, to prevent the glazing of the abrasive surface.

Grog: . . . . Clay which has been fired and then ground into granules of various particle sizes. Grog is added to clay bodies to reduce shrinkage after firing.

Hake brush: . . . . A natural fiber brush used in the application of shelf primer and other suspended materials because of its absorbent and retentive qualities.

Heat: . . . . A physical form of energy generated by combustion, electrical resistance, chemical action, or friction; heat is measured in calories or BTUs.

Heat soak: . . . . To maintain a specific kiln temperature for a given time; to be immersed (in heat) until thoroughly saturated.

Heat Transfer: . . . . The movement of heat from a warmer to a cooler body. Convection, conduction, and radiation are the methods of heat transfer. Convection is the transfer of heat through the movement of air currents. Conduction is the transfer of heat through contact with a warmer body. Radiation is the transfer of heat by means of electromagnetic waves given off by a glowing body.

High/medium/low switch: .... A switch used to control the flow of electrical current to the elements in a kiln. This switch is only used in a kiln which is equipped with two elements and is designed to power the elements in the following manner:

LOW — both elements are powered in series (each element putting out 25% of full power)

MEDIUM — only one element receives power (one element putting out 100% power)

HIGH — both elements receive power in parallel (both elements putting out 100% power)

Note: Where the output of this switch is constant, the output controlled by the infinite switch is cyclic.

Hydrated alumina: .... See **Alumina Hydrate.**

Idealized fusing cycle: .... A theoretical, simplified firing schedule made up of six stages: two for heating (initial heat, rapid heat) and four for cooling (rapid cool, anneal soak, anneal cool, cool to room temperature).

Incandescence: .... The emission of visible light by a hot object.

Inclusion: .... Any solid, liquid, or gaseous foreign body enclosed in glass.

Infinite switch: .... A type of temperature control with settings from 1 to 7 which determines the percentage of "on" time of the elements, thereby achieving the desired temperature level in the kiln.

Initial heat: .... The first stage of the Idealized Fusing Cycle during which the unfused layers of glass are heated from room temperature to just above the strain point. It is important that this stage be performed slowly to avoid cracking the glass.

Insulation brick: .... See **Soft Brick** (Also known as insulating firebrick.)

Iridizing solution: .... A metallic salt dissolved in a dilute hydrochloric acid solution that is sprayed onto the surface of very hot glass to produce a display of lustrous, rainbowlike colors. Stannous chloride is the most successful chemical used for the iridizing process. Other metal salts may be added to stannous chloride to provide an array of colors. The colors produced will depend upon the color and type of glass as well as how generously the chemical is applied. A good ventilation system is essential due to the production of dangerous vapors.

Tetra Iso Propyl Tytanate is a non-toxic, organic solution commonly used as an iridizing solution. However, it burns off in the fusing process, so is not practical for fused glass work.

Stannous Chloride Iridizing Solution

By volume:

1 part stannous (tin) chloride crystal
1 part muratic acid (swimming pool acid)
2 parts water

GLASSERY

The following metal salt proportions may replace 1 part stannous chloride:

Stannous chloride	.60	(Produces blue, green,
Ferric chloride	.40	and silver over dark colors.)
Stannous chloride	.70	(Produces blue over
Strontium nitrate	.15	amber glass.)
Barium chloride	.15	
Stannous chloride	.80	(Produces opalescent
Zinc chloride	.10	foggy white over most glasses)
Stannous chloride	.80	(Produces red shades
Ferric chloride	.10	over medium dark
Barium chloride	.05	glass.)
Strontium Nitrate	.05	

Kaolin: .... ($Al_2O_3 \cdot 2SiO_2 \cdot 2H_2O$) Commonly known as China clay, this is one type of clay which fires to a white color and has a pyrometric cone equivalent of 34-35; it is used as a major ingredient of shelf primer and a component of glass melting crucibles.

Kiln: .... Any of various ovens for hardening, burning, or drying substances; a brick-lined or fiber-insulated "oven" used to fuse glass or to bake or fire ceramics. Kilns used for glass and ceramics will reach temperatures from 1200 to 2400 degrees F.

Kiln sitter: .... A mechanical device that uses a small pyrometric cone to automatically shut off a kiln when the desired "heat work" has been accomplished. The kiln sitter is intended to assist in accurate firings and serve as a deterrent to over-firing. See **Cone.**

Kiln wash: .... See **Shelf Primer.**

Laminate: .... In glass fusing, the uniting of layers of glass without necessarily changing the original shape of the glass pieces (referred to as fuse-to-stick). Glass constructions, glued together, are often referred to as laminated.

Laminated safety glass: .... A composite of two sheets of float glass with a layer of transparent plastic in the middle, sandwiched together by the application of moderate heat and pressure.

Lampworking: .... The working and shaping of glass over a flame or a torch to cause flow.

Lavender oil: .... A light oil made from the lavender plant which is often used for a binder when applying enamels.

Lehr: .... A long, tunnel-shaped oven with a continuously moving belt or rollers which is designed for annealing, sagging, slumping, or for firing enamels or lusters on glass.

Luster: .... A suspension of metallic oxides in an organic solvent. Upon firing, the organic binders volitilize, leaving an extremely thin layer of metal oxides fused to the glass surface.

Malti: .... Italian glass tile.

Marinite: .... A high-duty refractory insulation board often used in place of a kiln shelf.

Marvering: .... The controlled forming of viscous glass on a flat metal table (marver). This technique is used in the making of color bars and in the glass blowing process.

Mature: . . . . A term used to describe the desired fired state of enamel, glaze, etc. If fired beyond the maturation point, it is said to be overfired; if below, underfired.

Metallic overglaze: . . . . See **Overglaze.** A metallic overglaze contains very fine particles of metal such as gold, silver, copper, or palladium. The result produced by firing these materials onto glass is a shiny, metallic surface (sometimes referred to as metallic luster).

Millefiore glass: . . . . Intricately arranged bundles of colored cane (frequently a floral pattern) fused together; pieces of this fused bundle (rod) are then used in other hot processes (e.g., fusing or the forming of the traditional millefiore paperweight).

Mold: . . . . A form in, over, or through which glass is shaped. A mold for glass forming must withstand temperatures of 1600 degrees F. and may be made of any refractory material, including clay, metal, or fiber.

Molten: . . . . Made liquid by heat; melted.

Mullion: . . . . A part of a window frame; a vertical strip dividing the panes of a window.

Mullite: . . . . Material with a high alumina content. When fired to 2600 degrees F., it will grow a specific mullite crystal that is very refractory and durable. Used commonly for kiln shelves, it has a smoother, less porous surface than silicon carbide and loses heat more quickly.

Nibbles: . . . . Hand-groused frit.

Opalescent glass: . . . . Translucent glass which exhibits a milky iridescence like that of an opal. The image of the incandescent light filament, transmitted through an opalescent glass, appears as a red outline.

Opaque: . . . . Impenetrable by light; neither transparent nor translucent.

Overglaze: . . . . A material composed of finely ground glass of a specific composition and applied to the pre-fused surface of the glass to prevent devitrification and to produce a very glassy surface. It is generally applied as a powder or suspended in a spray medium (such as Bullseye Spray "A").

Oxide: . . . . The compound formed by an element combined with oxygen. Glass is made by combining powdered oxides and melting or fusing them by the application of heat. The most important glass oxides are:

>> Silicon dioxide
>> Sodium oxide
>> Potassium oxide
>> Calcium oxide
>> Lead oxide.

Pate de verre: . . . . A process whereby crushed glass is fused in a mold.

Peephole: . . . . Any hole in a kiln with a plug which can be removed for observation. A peephole is NOT a vent!

Photo-sensitive glass: . . . . A type of glass where the development of images is dependent upon exposure to ultraviolet radiations, and later, heat treatment. The selective development of images is controlled by placing a mask or photographic film in contact with the glass before exposing it to ultraviolet radiations. In this way, photographs can be reproduced within the glass.

GLASSERY

Plate glass: .... A term often used to describe window glass which exceeds 3/16″ in thickness. All plate glass in the U.S.A. is presently made using the float process. In the past, plate glass was formed in a thicker sheet, ground to size, and polished.

Plate quality: .... A term referring to the quality of a glass which is uniform and optically true to the eye; originally, this term distinguished fine quality ground and polished plate glass from drawn sheet glass.

Plique-a-jour: .... An enameling technique which is similar to cloisonne without the metal base; thus, light passes through the enamel, forming a miniature stained glass window. The metal grid suspending the enamel is composed of bent wires (as in cloisonne), or it may be a solid piece of metal with holes pierced in it.

Polishing: .... This operation is carried on in a manner similar to grinding (see definition in 'Glassery'); however, the polishing material used is rouge (ferric oxide) or ceric oxide, both materials occurring in a finely powdered form. The polishing material is applied to a revolving buff which may be felt, leather, cork, etc. The action of polishing removes virtually no glass; it is currently theorized that a surface flow is produced which is confined to molecular dimensions in depth. In the case of optic polishing, very fine and accurate surfaces are produced.

Acid polishing is carried out by dipping the glass in a mixture of hydrofluoric and concentrated sulfuric acids. The acid polishes by reacting with the glass to lightly etch the surface. Due to the dangers of working with these acids, it is recommended for only the advanced or professional studio. It is **absolutely necessary** to have and utilize proper handling apparatus and a ventilated hood. (See list of supplies in the Appendix for names of professional studios that will acid polish glass works.)

Fire polishing or fire glazing is carried out by directing flames or radiant heat on the glass surface to cause surface flow.

Potentiometric: .... See **Pyrometer**.

Pressing: .... A method of shaping glass whereby force is applied to hot glass in a mold.

Punty: .... A solid steel gathering rod. A device to which glass is attached for holding during fire polishing or finishing.

Pyrex: .... A trademark name of borosilicate glass manufactured by Corning Glass Works. Pyrex has a low coefficient of expansion (approximately 33 to 36). Pyrex glass resists thermal shock when subjected to a direct flame.

Pyrometer: .... A device to measure temperature that is composed of three parts: a thermocouple, a temperature indicator, and a connecting lead wire. The indicator may be one of two types: galvanometric or potentiometric.

A galvonometric indicator is composed of a needle that rotates about a small shaft, indicating the temperature on a calibrated scale. Galvanometric devices do not require any external electrical power to operate, must be mounted in a vertical position and protected from abuse. Another characteristic of this type of device is that the lead length between the thermocouple and the indicator will affect the accuracy of the reading. These indicators are generally quite inexpensive.

A **potentiometric device** indicates the temperature on a digital display. Potentiometric indicators are more accurate but require electrical power to operate. Unlike the galvanometric device, the lead length between the thermocouple and the indicator does not affect the temperature reading. This type of indicator is generally more expensive than the galvanometric type.

Pyrometric Cone .... See **Cone.**

Quartz inversion: .... The slight re-arrangement of quartz crystals, accompanied by changes in volume, when the temperature of a clay body containing silica is raised to 1050 degrees F. This expansion upon heating is reversible upon cooling.

Radiant heat: .... Heat which is emitted by a glowing source such as a red-hot element in a kiln.

Rapid cool: .... The third stage of the Idealized Fusing Cycle where the fused glass is cooled from the highest temperature reached to the optimum annealing temperature.

Rapid heat: .... The second stage of the Idealized Fusing Cycle when the unfused layers of glass are heated from the strain point to the desired fused level.

Rebound: .... The phenomenon of returning heat to the kiln from heat stored in the kiln brick, insulation, or shelf after the rapid cool stage.

Refractories: .... Any of various materials such as alumina, silica, and zirconia that do not significantly deform or change chemically at high temperatures; may also refer to bricks of various shapes made of these materials and used to line furnaces and kilns.

Relief: .... The projection of figures or forms from a flat background to provide contours and contrast in shading and colors.

Renaissance: .... Generally, a period of revived intellectual or artistic achievement. Specifically, a period marked by the revival of classical art, literature, and learning which originated in Italy in the 14th century and later spread throughout Europe (through the 16th century).

Rolled glass: .... Sheet glass which is formed between two rollers or between one roller and a cast-iron table; produced primarily in the U.S.A.

Rouge: .... A reddish powder, chiefly ferric oxide, used to polish metals or glass.

Roughing: .... The act of creating a course, irregular surface in preparation for finishing and polishing; the first phase of grinding.

Safety glass: .... See **Laminated Safety Glass.**

Sagging: .... The downward sinking or bending of glass caused by its own unsupported weight while being heated; the cross section of the glass changes **noticeably** due to stretching. See SLUMPING.

Sandblasting: .... The use of a blast of air carrying sand at a high velocity to etch or cut glass or metal surfaces.

Saws: .... See **Saws** in list of supplies in Appendix.

Seed: .... An extremely small, gaseous inclusion in glass. 'Seedy' glass contains many bubbles, creating visual texture. When fusing above 1550 degrees F., seed bubbles rise to the surface and may cause blisters.

GLASSERY

Selenium colors: .... Selenium is a metallic element, black in powder form. Selenium, in conjunction with cadmium sulfide, creates glass colors ranging from amber orange to bright red. Selenium, by itself, will create a light rose color in soda lime glass. (Note: Selenium is a colloidal colorant and will often strike upon re-heating.)

Separator: .... See **Shelf Primer**.

Sgraffito: .... A technique of design ornamentation which employs a scratched line through a top layer of enamel, frit, etc., exposing the glass layer beneath (usually of a contrasting color).

Shard: .... A fragment of a brittle substance such as glass or ceramic. Shards are larger than frits.

Sheet fiber paper: .... See **Fiber Paper**.

Shelf primer: .... (Also known as kiln wash and glass separator.) This material is a mixture of hydrated alumina and china clay, binders, and suspension agents. Its purpose is to keep glass from sticking to glass forming or fusing surfaces. (See Chapter 3.)

Siccative: .... A medium which promotes the drying of oils used on underglaze or overglaze colors.

Silicon carbide: .... (SiC) A bluish-black crystalline compound (one of the hardest known substances) used as an abrasive or refractory material; it is also frequently used in rough grinding. Shelves made of silicon carbide are used for high-fire ceramics, but are generally too rough for glass fusing.

Silk-screening: .... A method of producing a stencil with which a design is imposed upon a screen of silk or other fine fabric; blank areas are coated with an impermeable substance, and a printing medium is forced through the cloth onto the printing surface.

Single strength glass: .... Clear window glass which is 3/32″ thick.

Sinter: .... To fire to the point where cohesion of the material begins.

Slumping: .... The controlled bending or downward sinking of glass while being heated; unlike sagging, the cross section of a slumped piece does **not** change noticeably.

Slump method: .... A testing method to determine the proper annealing range of specific glasses (if this information is not available from the manufacturer). (See "Testing Glass for Determination of the Annealing Range," Chapter 7.)

Soak: .... See **Heat Soak**.

Sodium silicate: .... ($Na_2SiO_3 \cdot 9H_2O$) Often referred to as "water glass," sodium silicate is water soluble and occurs as a white powder or a liquid of different viscosities; used as a binder in refractory mold mixes and as a low-temperature flux.

Soft brick: .... A porous refractory brick used to insulate kilns (also known as insulating firebrick). These bricks can be carved with a file, knife, or sandpaper. If coated with shelf primer, soft brick may be used for molds.

Softening point: .... See **Fiber Softening Point**.

Squeegee oil: .... A fluid composed of pine oil and solvent which is available in various viscosities; used for silk-screening and frit application in fused glass work.

Stone: .... An imperfection in glass; may be a piece of furnace brick or crystalline contaminations in glass.

Strain: .... The deformation (change in dimension) of a body of glass due to stress.

Strain point: .... The temperature at which the internal stresses are reduced to low values in 4 hours. At this point, the glass is substantially rigid. The data for determining the strain point are compiled using the same procedures used for the determination of the annealing point, but for a slower rate of fiber elongation (see **Annealing Point.**)

Strength of glass: .... The capacity of glass to resist damage from outside forces. Generally, thicker glass or glass which has been exposed to specific chemical or heat treatment will exhibit increased strength.

Stress: .... The force which tends to deform or strain a glass body. Stress is a force per unit area, usually expressed in pounds per square inch. Strain in glass is the result of stress. The two main types of stress existing in glass are compressive and tensile stress: tension resulting from stretching; compression resulting from squeezing.

Stressometer: .... The name given to the small polarimeter distributed by the Fusing Ranch. The Stressometer is a light source with one diffusing lens and two polarized lenses, which when properly used, will give a visual indication of the amount of stress existing in two glasses which have been fused together. (See Chapter 5.)

Stria: .... A cord of low intensity, usually used in reference to antique glass. Reamey antique glass has striae created by gathering glasses of different viscosities before forming and blowing. Striae sometimes may be seen in clear glass when viewed on a Stressometer or polarimeter; these striae are created by immiscible glasses.

Striking: .... The term referring to the re-heating of glass after cooling to develop color or opacity when glass contains colloidal particles. This re-heating above 1100 degrees F. causes very small particles in the glass matrix to grow larger or to migrate together. This is referred to as striking.

Stringer: .... A fine, very thin glass thread (less than 1/16" in diameter). Stringers are often a by-product of glass casting; they may also be made by dipping a punty in molten glass and whipping it from side to side. Stringers may be made from flat glass scraps by using a torch and a pair of pliars. They are often used in fusing for fine detail work. Glass rods are usually straighter and larger than stringers.

Stringer glass: .... Sheet glass containing stringers cast into the underside of hand-cast sheets to refract light and add line quality.

Stylus: .... A sharply pointed instrument used for marking or engraving.

Suspension .... A relatively course, non-colloidal dispersion of solid particles in a liquid.

Temperature: .... The intensity of heat as measured in degrees Fahrenheit or Centigrade. (See Temperature Conversion Chart in Appendix.)

GLASSERY

Tempering Glass: . . . . A treatment given to glass to produce internal stress by sudden cooling from low red heat. When the glass surface is cooled suddenly with a blast of air (1-2 minutes), the surface hardens rapidly and becomes rigid. As the cooling continues, the inner part of the glass continues to shrink, causing the outer surface to be in compression. This makes the glass very tough. Tempered glass cannot be cut; attempting to do so will cause the glass to break into tiny pieces.

Glass that has been rapidly cooled from near the softening point, under rigorous control, to increase its mechanical and thermal endurance, is referred to as tempered glass.

Teracotta: . . . . A clay used in pottery and building construction which is reddish-brown in color.

Tessera: . . . . Small pieces of glass or other material. Tesserae usually refers to squares or the individual elements of a mosaic piece.

Thermal endurance: . . . . The relative ability of glassware to withstand thermal shock.

Thermal shock: . . . . Shock pertaining to, or caused by, heat. Thermal cracking occurs in glass as a result of too-rapid heating or cooling below the strain point temperature of the glass.

Thermocouple: . . . . A thermoelectric device used to measure temperature accurately, especially one consisting of two dissimilar metals joined at one end so that a potential difference generated between the junction of the two metals is a measure of the temperature.

There are many types of thermocouples. The most commonly used for measuring temperatures in the fusing range is type "K," which is composed of the two metal alloys known as chromel and alumel. The junction is welded together and ceramic spacers are used to insulate the two wires from each other. As the temperature of the junction increases, the voltage between the two leads, A and B, increases. This voltage is what drives the meter. The meter actually reads millivolts; however, for convenience, this has already been converted to degrees on the dial face.

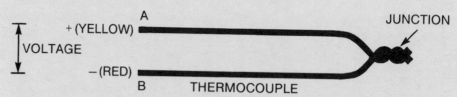

In the case of the potentiometric device, the indicator generates an equal and opposite current to cause zero flow of electricity between thermocouple and indicator. It is this current amount that is displayed as the equivalent temperature reading.

Tin oxide: . . . . (SnO) A white powder used for polishing glass.

Translucent: . . . . Transmitting light, but causing sufficient diffusion to eliminate perception of distinct images.

Transparent: . . . . Capable of transmitting light so that objects or images may be seen as if there were no intervening material.

Tungsten carbide: .... (WC) An extremely hard, fine gray powder used in tools, dies, wear-resistant machine parts, and abrasives; used for rough grinding.

Vent: .... An opening, serving as an outlet for air, smoke, fumes and the like. Kilns are vented to allow fumes from organic material to escape during early heat-up and to allow excess heat to escape after reaching fusing temperature. (Note: A peephole is not a vent.)

Viscosity: .... The measure of resistance of a liquid to flow. As the viscosity increases, the liquid becomes stiffer. Viscosity is measured in centipoises. In glass, viscosity increases as the temperature decreases; therefore, glass becomes stiffer and stiffer as it cools until the temperature is below the strain point, at which time it is so stiff that it acts as a solid.

Vitreous: .... Pertaining to, resembling, or having the nature of glass; the glassy state.

Volatile: .... Evaporating rapidly; passing off readily into gasous form. When organic binders and wetting agents (such as white glue and squeegee oil) are heated above 500 degrees F., they volatilize, creating the need to vent the fusing kiln.

Warp: .... A slight bend or twist in a straight or flat form. Warping in fused glass occurs due to improper annealing or the use of incompatible glasses. (See "Testing for Compatibility," Chapter 5.)

Water glass: .... See **Sodium Silicate.**

Whiting: .... See **Calcium Carbonate.**

Working range: .... A temperature range in which glass may be formed. The "upper end" refers to an elevated temperature at which glass may be readily moved with tools, while the "lower end" refers to the temperature at which it is sufficiently viscous to hold its formed shape. Slumping takes place at the lower end of the working range, while combing is possible at the middle to upper end of the working range.

NOTES

NOTES

NOTES

NOTES

NOTES

NOTES

Your response to the questions below will be appreciated and will insure you of being included on a mailing list to receive updates on fusing information, as we are able to make new ideas available. Please return this page with your answers to:

VITREOUS PUBLICATIONS, INC.
3625 S.E. 21st Avenue
Portland, Oregon 97202

1) How did you learn of this book? _____

2) Did you find information in this book to which you had not previously been exposed?

_____
_____

3) What was the most helpful part of the book?

_____
_____
_____

4) In order for this book to meet your needs did you find that any aspect of glass fusing was overlooked?

_____
_____
_____

5) Do you need more information on any of the following?
☐ Equipment   ☐ Technical Information
☐ Sources of Supply   ☐ Available Classes
☐ Molds/Molding   ☐ Other (list below)
☐ How to Teach Fusing
_____

6) Are you presently teaching some form of glass working?

No _____ Yes _____ Type _____

7) Other than fusing, what, if any, are your interests in glass working?
☐ Glass Blowing   ☐ Lampwork   ☐ Leading and Foiling
☐ Bevelling   ☐ Sandblasting and Etching

8) Is your present involvement in glass work as a:
☐ Studio Artist   ☐ Retailer of supplies
  ☐ Ceramics   ☐ Hobbyist
  ☐ Glass   ☐ Teacher in art school or art department

Name of school: _____

NAME _____

STUDIO OR BUSINESS NAME _____

ADDRESS _____

CITY _____ STATE _____ ZIP _____

TELEPHONE _____